Recovery from Trauma with Psychosynthesis Psychotherapy

Soul Trauma and the Story of Persephone

Linda Hoyle, PhD

To Jane
Love from Linda

Copyright © 2018 by Linda Hoyle

All rights reserved. No part of this book, except for brief quotations embodied in critical articles and reviews, may be reproduced, stored in a retrieval system or transmitted in any form or by any means - electronic, mechanical, photocopying, recording, or otherwise - without the prior written permission of the publisher.

Published by
Linda Hoyle, PhD
Felmersham, Bedford, England, UK
www.lindahoyle.co.uk

Cover photo © Linda Hoyle
Abduction of Persephone, painting on the Piccolomini Library ceiling in the Doumo di Siena, Italy

ISBN: 978-1-731-51153-9

CONTENTS

List of Diagrams and Tables .... *iv*
Acknowledgements .... *v*
About the Author .... *vii*
Introduction *1*

PART ONE
THEORETICAL BACKGROUND

Chapter One	Psychosynthesies Context	7
	Assagioli: Psychological System	7
	Evans: Psychotherapeutic Framework	11
	Levels of Wounding	12
	Triphasic Model	21
	Soul Trauma	24

PART TWO
BRINGING THEORY TO LIFE

Chapter Two	The Story of Persephone	33
Chapter Three	Clinical Case Study	35
	Client Biography	35
	Presenting Issues	36
	3.1 Pre-personal Level	37
	3.2 Personal Level	43
	3.3 Transpersonal Level	50
Chapter Four	Conclusion	61

Bibliography *67*
Other Books by this Author *71*

LIST OF DIAGRAMS AND TABLES

Diagram 1	Assagioli's Psychological System	8
Diagram 2	Triphasic Model (Evans, 2013)	23
Diagram 3	Movement from Neurotic to Existential guilt/shame	53
Diagram 4	Parallels between the journey of Persephone and Mary	62
Table 1	Summary of Pre-personal Level	42
Table 2	Summary of Personal Level	49
Table 3	Strategies for Self-soothing and Grounding	56
Table 4	Summary of Transpersonal Level	60

ACKNOWLEDGEMENTS

I am indebted to my clients who have taught me so much about how to work with them and also for their invaluable feedback about what does not work. Quite frankly I would not have been able to write this book without their help.

I am grateful for my training at the Institute of Psychosynthesis and to all the tutors and supervisors who have grounded my theoretical understanding and supported my practice. In particular, my heartfelt thanks go to Joan Evans as my MA thesis tutor. Her thorough guidance, expertise and creativity have been inspirational. I have included references in this book to tutorials that I had with Joan during 2018 when she shared her developing ideas about psychosynthesis theory and practice. Joan supported me to write my thesis for an MA in Psychosynthesis Psychotherapy and I received The Emma Stavrou Thesis Award. This book is based on the foundations of my MA thesis, which I have edited to make accessible to a wider readership.

My thanks also go to Roger Evans, Mickey Kaufmann and Debbie Friedman, who have been incredibly influential in my learning and development as a psychosynthesis practitioner. I am also grateful to Adrian Bickers who was my training psychotherapist. Personally, I learn best from experience. Being a client with Adrian was not only life changing, in terms of my personal development, but it was also powerful for me to witness a highly skilful psychosynthesis psychotherapist at work.

My husband Tim has been amazing in his support and patience while I completed my psychosynthesis training and in writing this book. I am grateful for his practical guidance, encouragement and love.

Finally, my thanks go to my good friends Carol Stork and Maria Hood who have read drafts, given me valuable feedback and inspired me to keep resilient.

ABOUT THE AUTHOR

Linda Hoyle, BSc (Hons), MA, PhD, Dip.Psychotherapy, C.Psychol., AFBPsS

Linda is a BACP & UKCP accredited psychotherapist and chartered psychologist working in private practice in Bedford, England, UK. She specialises in supporting adults who are feeling lost and anxious due to major transitions and crisis in their life. She has a Diploma and MA in Psychosynthesis Psychotherapy from the Institute of Psychosynthesis and Middlesex University and is a qualified EMDR therapist. Linda has worked with clients who have experienced trauma, either as a series of events throughout their childhood/adulthood or as a single event.

Before establishing her private practice as a psychotherapist, Linda was founder and Managing Director of Workplace Potential Ltd. She was part of a team that provided leadership coaching, group facilitation and leadership development programmes across a broad spectrum of organisations. Previous to that, Linda was a Principal Consultant and Director of Development Programmes at the Tavistock Consultancy (Tavistock & Portman NHS Trust).

Linda has been an academic tutor for counselling students, and a trainer for leadership coaches. She provides supervision to counsellors, therapists and leadership coaches and is a member of the British Psychological Society (BPS) register of Applied Psychology Practice Supervisors. Linda is an Associate Fellow of the BPS and a Chartered Member of the BPS Special Group in Coaching Psychology.

Linda's PhD in psychology was a psychoanalytic and systems model perspective on understanding and overcoming resistance to organisational change. Her work on the leadership of change has been published and she has lectured on this topic at masters and doctoral level.

www.lindahoyle.co.uk

INTRODUCTION

There has been a refreshing movement in recent years with increased public interest and scientific research focused on understanding the devastating impact that traumatic events have on people. On a daily basis the media brings into our homes the most horrendous personal stories of individuals who have experienced historical childhood abuse, violence, sexual assault, serious accidents or terrorism. We bear witness to images of children and adults who are being displaced from their homes due to natural disasters or acts of war. At last it is being widely acknowledged that traumatic events such as these have a huge impact on individuals and can produce serious, long lasting psychological effects.

The world of treatment for survivors of trauma has begun to move away from pathological diagnosis, which only served to burden more shame on the victim and reinforce their reluctance to be visible with their suffering. A breath of fresh air has blown away the cobwebs of traditional 'talking cure' psychotherapy where well-intentioned therapists inadvertently re-traumatised their clients by encouraging them to retell and re-experience the trauma of their story. Advances in neuroscience and the scientific study of effective treatments for trauma recovery are uncovering how individuals develop an amazing array of defensive coping mechanisms to protect themselves from the impact of trauma. This research has improved our understanding about how people can use their own natural, in-built self-healing processes to recover from trauma; literally recovering from the inside out.

Psychosynthesis has at its heart the idea that individuals recover from the inside out. Established in the mid 1960's and based on the work of Roberto Assagioli, psychosynthesis has evolved over time in line with advances in therapeutic knowledge and practice. The integrative nature of the psychosynthesis approach allows inclusion of the neuroscience evidence about how the brain and nervous system are impacted by trauma and can incorporate innovative ways of working somatically with traumatised clients.

In this book I offer an in-depth understanding of the theory and practice of the psychosynthesis approach that can be used to help individuals recover from Soul Trauma (Evans, 2007). The term Soul Trauma is used to describe the experience for some individuals when the beginning of life is chronically traumatic. This can range from consistent emotional neglect, abandonment and rejection through to more extreme incidents such as violence, sexual abuse, displacement, repeated medical procedures, serious illness and accidents.

I will outline Soul Trauma in more detail and use a clinical case study to describe the psychotherapeutic process used in psychosynthesis, which is known as the Triphasic Model of Psychospiritual Unfoldment (Evans, 2013). I will also refer to the story of Persephone, which is a Greek myth about a young woman who experiences Soul Trauma and then goes on a journey of recovery. I make connections between the characters, i.e. archetypes, in the story and the clinical case study. This comparison shows how trauma impacts an individual and what the process of recovery looks like.

Guidance on How to Read this Book

This book is intended for two types of readers. Firstly, for readers who are interested in the in-depth theory of psychosynthesis and how it is applied to client work, e.g. students of psychosynthesis, or practitioners such as counsellors, psychotherapists and coaches. Secondly, readers from a lay-person perspective who may have a personal interest in understanding their own recovery from trauma, would like to see what psychosynthesis therapy would be like as a client or have a curiosity about the parallels between recovery from trauma and the myth of Persephone.

My suggestion for the first group of readers, students and practitioners, is that they may like to begin with Part One, the theoretical background. In Chapter One I set out the psychosynthesis context of theory and therapeutic practice that can be used with clients who have experienced childhood trauma. The purpose of this is to be clear about how a psychosynthesis approach provides a psychospiritual context compared to traditional psychodynamic approaches.

Introduction

I will outline the seminal work of Roberto Assagioli (1965, 1974 & 1988) who formulated a psychological system for transpersonal development under the name psychosynthesis. I then describe the contribution of Evans (2007 & 2013) who developed a psychosynthesis psychotherapeutic framework. I will cover the three core components of Levels of Wounding, Triphasic Model of Psychospiritual Unfoldment, and Soul Trauma. Reading this chapter will provide a thorough grounding for students and practitioners to proceed through the remaining chapters of the book.

My suggestion for the second group of readers, from a layperson perspective, would be to begin with Part Two, bringing theory to life. In Chapter Two I describe the Greek myth of Persephone and her mother Demeter, which provides archetypes to understand Soul Trauma and the clinical case study. This gives a good grounding for the reader to proceed to Chapter Three where I link details from the clinical case to the archetypes in the myth and illustrate how the client material connects to Soul Trauma.

The clinical case study is described in Chapter Three, which is divided into sections focusing on the three different levels of the psychosynthesis Triphasic Model of recovery (Evans, 2013). The levels are known as the pre-personal level, personal level and transpersonal level. Each level is described and illustrated with examples of how the client presents, what the dynamics look like in the relationship between the client and therapist, and what key interventions are used in the therapeutic process. Of course, the reader is welcome at any time to dip back into the theory section in Part One if they would like a more thorough understanding of key concepts that are mentioned throughout the book.

In Chapter Four I conclude with a summary of themes from the clinical case study that illustrate how the Triphasic Model can be used as an effective therapeutic framework by psychotherapists to understand and work with Soul Trauma clients.

Confidentiality of Clinical Case Material

The examples I have used for the clinical case study are drawn from my therapy work with a number of women and men who have experienced Soul Trauma. To protect my clients' anonymity and respect confidentiality, I have created one composite clinical case study based on a wide range of material. I have done my best to disguise the identity of any individuals and any similarities to actual people or events are not intentional.

The clinical case also includes material from my personal story. I experienced chronic trauma during early infancy and my recovery has involved nearly 30 years of different therapeutic approaches. I bring to this book examples from both sides of the psychosynthesis therapeutic relationship; being a client and a therapist.

I have named the client Mary and the vignettes I have created serve the purpose to illustrate:

a) how the therapist can recognise that a client is presenting with Soul Trauma;

b) what it is like for clients to experience Soul Trauma;

c) how the client and therapist experience the process at the three different levels during psychosynthesis therapy, i.e. pre-personal, personal and transpersonal;

d) what outcomes can happen during different stages of the psychosynthesis therapeutic process.

Having regular professional supervision as a therapist is essential support and promotes self care. This enables the therapist to step back from the client material, receive feedback, examine the unconscious material communicated by the client and understand the work from a different perspective. I have included some examples of feedback I received during supervision that has shone a much-needed light on the complex dynamics of the therapeutic relationship.

PART ONE

THEORETICAL BACKGROUND

1. PSYCHOSYNTHESIS CONTEXT

The psychosynthesis context that I am using in this book has been developed over the last 40 years by Joan and Roger Evans (Evans, 2007) who founded the Institute of Psychosynthesis, London. Their work builds on the seminal ideas of Roberto Assagioli (1965, 1974 & 1988) who formulated a psychological system for transpersonal development under the name psychosynthesis.

Assagioli initially trained as a psychoanalyst and first published his ideas about the bio-psychospiritual reality of the human being in 1909. In this chapter I outline the psychological system developed by Assagioli and then focus on key ideas developed by Evans that are relevant to my book.

Assagioli: Psychological System

The term transpersonal was used by Assagioli "to refer to what is commonly called spiritual ... in that it refers to that which is beyond or above the ordinary personality" (1988, p12). He used the term spiritual to include "not only specifically religious experiences, but all states of consciousness, all those functions and activities which pertain to values above the norm: ethical, aesthetic, heroic, humanitarian and altruistic" (ibid., p13).

Assagioli preferred to use a scientific approach to study the awakening and development of spiritual consciousness beginning with the facts and experiences, and then progressing to the interpretation of what has been observed and discovered (ibid., p16). He devised a psychological system in diagram form to illustrate the "constitution of the human being in his living concrete reality" (Assagioli, 1965, p16). Although this appears structural and one dimensional it is intended to illustrate the dynamic movement and interplay of how an individual becomes conscious of different levels of experience (see Diagram 1).

Diagram 1: Assagioli's Psychological System

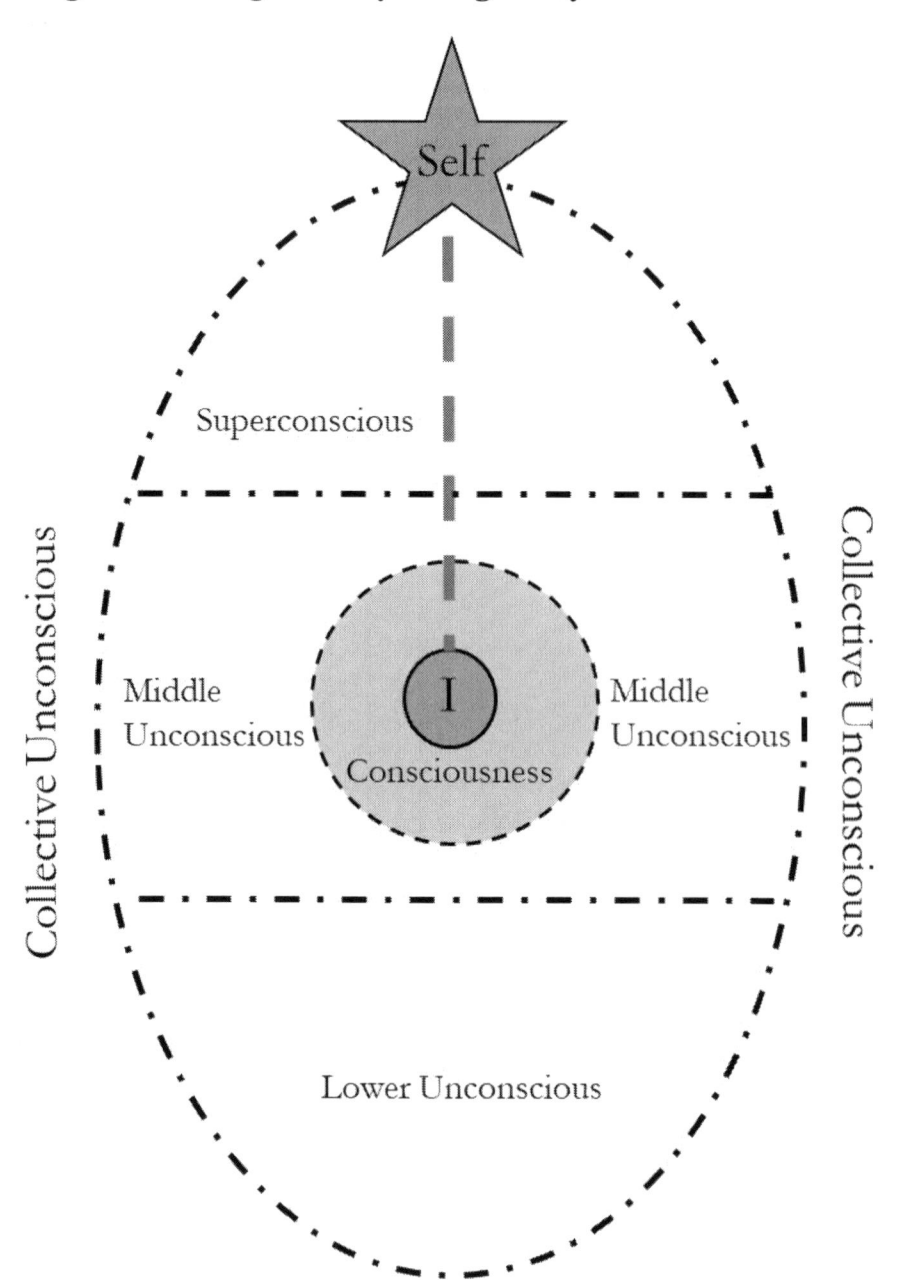

Self

Superconscious

Collective Unconscious

Middle Unconscious

I

Consciousness

Middle Unconscious

Collective Unconscious

Lower Unconscious

At the centre of the psychological system is the conscious 'I' and field of consciousness. This represents the individual having the capacity to become aware, i.e. conscious, of a variety of experiences. For example, the person would say to themselves or to others "I am aware of ..." or "I am conscious of..." This follows Asssagioli's preference to begin with the human experience followed by interpretation of what has been discovered. As the field of consciousness expands the individual widens their experience at the levels of the middle unconscious, the lower unconscious, the collective unconscious, and the superconscious.

The middle unconscious refers to experiences that are close to the field of conscious awareness, such as competencies that are necessary for everyday tasks but require a low level of conscious energy. For example, when we become proficient at driving a car it is quite normal to drive for a long journey without being aware of changing gears and observing traffic to the point that we can be thinking of other things or hold a conversation. However, when there is sudden danger on the road our necessary competencies come into sharp focus within our field of 'I' consciousness to ensure we remain safe.

The lower unconscious refers to experiences from the individual's history that they have repressed using ego defence mechanisms. It is important to note that repression is a necessary survival coping strategy used by the individual to deal with experiences that were too painful to bear at the time. According to Assagioli (1965, p17) the lower unconscious consists of primitive drives, urges, complexes, dreams and imagination of an inferior kind as well as lower level psychic experiences such as phobias, obsessions, compulsions and paranoid delusions.

Although traditionally the lower unconscious has been the focus for psychoanalysts, it is also essential for the work of psychosynthesis psychotherapists. By holding a psychosynthesis context an individual client can be guided to expand their field of conscious 'I' awareness to include contents of the lower unconscious. This is known as pre-personal ego development and will be outlined in more detail later.

Jung (1969) made a distinction between the contents of the personal (lower) unconscious, which have at some time been conscious and then repressed, and the contents of the collective unconscious, which he believed owe their existence exclusively to heredity. He proposed that the collective unconscious is made up of archetypes, which seem to have been present always and everywhere. Jung proposed that these universal mental images or thought forms can be seen across myths, fairytales, in personal dreams and visions across different cultures (ibid.).

For Assagioli (1988) the main focus of study was the individual experience of the superconscious and his research documented two ways that can happen. The most frequently experienced was 'descendant': "the bursting in of superconscious elements into the conscious mind in the form of intuitive thoughts, sudden enlightenment or inspiration" (ibid. p20). The second he described as 'ascendant': "raising our centre of consciousness, the self-conscious 'I', to levels above the ordinary until we reach the sphere of the superconscious" (ibid. p21). He described thirteen characteristics of the superconscious:

- Depth – reaching the source of one's being, leaving behind ordinary level of consciousness
- Internalization – moving to the centre of one's being
- Elevation – rising up to a higher level
- Path – having a sense of a road that must be travelled
- Expansion – overriding boundaries of the separate 'I'; and sense of being part of a greater consciousness
- Activation – being freed from what hinders us and being able to emerge
- Empowering - feeling stronger, dynamic and fullness
- Awakening – having a sense of moving from dreamlike state to enhanced alertness
- Joy – having a sense of happiness
- Bliss - having a sense of peaceful stillness
- Regeneration – birth of a new state of being
- Resurrection – rising up of a state that had been lost
- Liberation – having a sense of inner freedom

Assagioli (1988) made an important distinction between the superconscious and the spiritual Self, which appears as a star at the top of his diagram of the psychological system (see Diagram 1). Although the contents of the superconscious are close in characteristics to the Self the difference is that the superconscious contents are active, dynamic and changing. In contrast, the Self is "stable, unmoving, unchanging, and for this reason is different" (ibid., p26). Assagioli illustrates the alignment between 'I' and Self with a connecting line on his diagram. He described how the sense of permanence and stability of the Self is transmitted to its counterpart, the conscious personal 'I', which "gives us our sense of permanence and personal identity throughout all the changes, alternating states of mind and changing contents of our awareness" (ibid., p26).

This is important because Assagioli proposed that the Self identifies with different parts of the personality, i.e. subpersonalities, different roles in life, and with body, feelings and mind. He is clear that "however much we identify ourselves with different 'roles' ... we know that we are always ourselves" (ibid., p26). Assagioli emphasised that "the self awareness of the conscious 'I' is only a poor reflection of the enduring, immortal essence of the spiritual Self" (ibid., p26). Assagioli (1965) developed the term 'disidentification' to describe the capacity that an individual can practice keeping a psychological distance from being over identified with a particular 'role', feeling, thought or body sensation. He created various exercises and techniques which were intended to enable individuals to develop their capacity for disidentification (ibid.)

Assagioli (1988) placed the Self on the periphery of his diagram of the psychological system to indicate it has a dual nature. He considered the Self to be partly inside the individual psychological system in a continuous relationship with the superconscious and partly outside, indicating that Self is both individual and universal at the same time. He described this position as a state of consciousness that can be experienced as heightened awareness, limitless expansion, intense joy and bliss, and a sublime experience (ibid.). This concept of the Self being both individual and universal was a key idea developed further by Evans (2007) and will be covered in the next section.

Evans: Psychotherapeutic Framework

The contribution of Evans (2007) was to build on Assagioli's psychological system and develop a psychotherapeutic framework for psychosynthesis practitioners to use with clients.

In this section I will cover three core components of this psychotherapeutic framework that are relevant to my book and these are Levels of Wounding, Triphasic Model of Psychospiritual Unfoldment, and Soul Trauma.

Levels of Wounding

The psychotherapeutic model developed by Evans (2007) is known as 'Soulmaking at Work' and so it is important in this section to differentiate between what is meant by the terms **the Self** and **the soul**. I will firstly outline a definition of the Self, then describe the sacred wound, which leads to a definition of the soul. Then I will outline the primal wound and existential wound.

The Self
Linking back to Assagioli's definition of the Self as being both individual and universal at the same time, this is developed by Evans (2007) who makes it clear that the spiritual Self and the embodied Self are all one thing. Evans (2007) uses the term 'transpersonal Self' to refer to the 'spiritual Self'. For consistency, from now on I will also refer to the 'transpersonal Self'.

According to Evans, the Self is both everything and also the Self is no-thing (ibid.). In order to become something, in other words to know itself, the Self incarnates and builds around itself a body, i.e. Self becomes embodied. "The intention to incarnate is registered at the level of Being, i.e. the Self" (Evan, 2007, Vol 4, p7). "The act of incarnation is the process whereby the Being engages in and with the world, i.e. the 'I' is the Self at the level of embodiment" (ibid., p7).

While Assagioli (1965) admits that he left out the essential dynamic of the will from his diagram of the psychological system, Evans is clear that the 'I' is both the vehicle for consciousness and the will in our embodied life (2007, p8). Assagioli does write separately about the will in his book 'The Act of Will' (1974) and describes that "the will has a *directive* and *regulatory* function; it balances and constructively utilizes all other activities and energies of the human being without repressing any of them" (ibid., p10).

Sacred Wound
Evans uses the phrase the sacred wound to describe incarnation as the experience of "an act of separation of the part 'I' from the whole Self" (2017, p1). The newly incarnated infant experiences this with such deep trauma and suffering and loses consciousness of the whole Self. As the infant becomes unconscious of Self, they are left feeling "bewildered and lost in a world not of [their] own making" (ibid., p1). The sacred wound is "the wound of incarnation, which cannot be healed only suffered" (ibid., p1). The

suffering at the level of sacred wounding brings anxiety, betrayal, alienation and abandonment, which increases as the infant grows up, interacts more with the outer world and journey's further away from the Self (ibid.). The experience of the sacred wound brings with it a deep sense of loss of the whole, loss of meaning and loss of purpose "which triggers the will to return through the experience of 'Divine Homesickness' – the thrust towards wholeness" (ibid., p1).

Evans (2018) makes it clear that the Self is not something that sits in the spiritual realm, but that the Self is the whole thing and not separated from that which is embodied. It is the Self which is embodied and expresses itself through identification with body, feelings, mind and personality. Self awareness is part of the process of embodment and it is within the body that Self awakens and becomes aware of itself (ibid.).

The Soul

According to Evans (2007) the soul is the individual's experience of Self embodiment, i.e. the soul is the medium of experience. This is in contrast to the popular use of the word 'soul' as being personal, e.g. when someone refers to 'my soul'. Evans (ibid.) states that within a psychosynthesis context the soul is not personal, i.e. not a part of the individual, but rather that the medium of 'the soul' gives rise to an individual having a personal experience that is soulful. In this way it is different to the Self. The soul can only be known by direct experience and is often sensed as feelings and knowing, which can be difficult to understand rationally or express verbally (ibid.).

When an individual has an experience of the realm of the soul, they have greater access to the superconscious, which brings them into connection with Self (Evans, 2018). In this way, the realm of the soul holds a relationship and bridging towards the Self. A clear example would be situations of public grief, such as the annual Remembrance Service marking the death of armed forces personnel during military combat. The level of gravitas and ceremony that is designed into such a ritual brings an opportunity for people to have a soulful experience, to gain greater access to the superconscious and connection to Self. Evans is clear that such rituals serve the awakening of the soul at an individual level, but that the experience of the soul is not individual, i.e. the soul can be experienced collectively (ibid.).

It is important to make this distinction because a fundamental part of psychosynthesis psychotherapy is to guide the client into the realm of the soul, so that they have an experience that then frees the will to evolve and develop. This is what is meant by the term 'Soulmaking at Work' and the psychosynthesis therapist is often known as 'the midwife of the soul' (Evans, 2007). In a similar way to how the organisers carefully design the ritual of a Remembrance Service, a key part of the role of the psychosynthesis therapist is to energise the realm of soul in their relationship with clients so that there is greater access to the superconscious (Evans, 2018).

In contrast, it is possible to have an experience that is 'soulless'. I illustrate this with a real-life situation. Imagine you are part of a group of friends who love ballroom dancing. You plan a trip to the Tower Ballroom in Blackpool and buy tickets for afternoon tea at the weekly tea dance. You anticipate an inspiring and elegant experience and dress up for the occasion. You arrive at your allocated time at reception and are asked to join a long queue that runs parallel to the ballroom. The corridor is narrow with walls either side, but you are near an entrance that gives you a chance to see into the ballroom. The room is squeezed full of hundreds of people. Couples attempt to dance on the packed dancefloor but bump into each other. Small tables for afternoon tea are jammed into the room so that people are sitting shoulder to shoulder. The temperature is roasting hot. The only person with any space is the man playing the Wurlitzer Organ on the stage.

The 'entrance' you are standing next to is really the 'exit'. People leaving the ballroom push through the crowds in the queue. Suddenly, another door opens near that exit and staff bring trolleys of clean crockery through the queue ready to clear the tables. They return with trolleys full of dirty dishes. Families with young children become hungry and restless. The noise, chaos and heat become unbearable. The queue does not move. You have been waiting for an hour. There is no communication from staff and finally you find someone who admits that the computer system had been faulty resulting in overbooking – more tickets were sold than they have capacity to manage.

On hearing this you return to reception, demand your money back and once that transaction is complete you leave the Ballroom feeling disappointed, angry and hungry. This collective experience for the group, and perhaps all participants, could be described as soulless. The organisers of the tea dance lacked any kind of effective management function and did not take care to create a soulful experience; people did not gain greater access to the superconscious and connection to Self. The motivation for the organisers seemed to be about making as much revenue as possible.

In contrast, the Remembrance Service in London involves thousands of people and the management function of the organisers is impeccable. They design the event in such a way as to evoke the imagination of participants. Stories are told, pictures and shown, haunting music is played, and bloodshed on the battle fields is represented by the poppy garlands. Then silence provides a space for the imagination of participants to connect them to the realm of the soul. Thousands of service men and women march past the Cenotaph in a moving display of belongingness and respect for those who died in conflict.

In order to fully participate in such a soulful experience, individuals need to have a rich inner ground of emotions and the Remembrance Service provides a range of sensations to evoke the imaginal world. In the same way, clients need to have a rich ground of inner emotions to access the realm of the soul. It is part of the role of psychosynthesis therapists to build the imaginal world with clients, to enable them to develop a rich ground in their inner emotional world to access the realm of the soul (Evans, 2018).

The therapist needs to have an effective management function to be able to design and create safe boundaries, give appropriate structure to the therapeutic space and manage the process impeccably. This enables the client to build their imaginal world, and with it access to the soul and superconscious. The client comes more into relationship internally with Self and at the same time builds their relationship with the external world. The more the imaginal world develops within the individual, they increase their desire and begin to see what they want. This in turn increases their field of will, i.e. the more they can imagine what they desire, the more they want this to happen, and the more their will evolves (ibid.).

The soul can be directly experienced by the therapist and the client, but only if both individuals are willing and ready to open themselves up to their own sense of Being. Many clients who seek therapy are out of touch with their inner world of emotions and this has impoverished their capacity to experience the soul (Evans, 2018). They may have a personal history where they were not educated in their experience and understanding of feelings or they have repressed emotions in order to survive an unbearable level of physical or emotional pain.

Such an individual, who is unable to access the realm of soul, lacks a bridge to the superconscious and connection to Self, which blocks the opportunity for the will to develop and evolve (ibid.). It is likely the individual has experienced primal wounding, and this is outlined in the next section.

Primal Wound

As described earlier, the infant experiences the sacred wound. The Self incarnates and 'I' is unconscious in an infant embodied state that is still too small and vulnerable to be effective at fulfilling its purpose in the world (Evans, 2018). Outside of the womb the infant takes many years to grow to full emotional and cognitive maturity and the infant Self is initially identified with bodily sensations. The Self makes an unconscious choice to identify with the ego and the 'I' goes unconscious (ibid.).

The use of the term 'ego' has a different meaning in the context of psychological theory compared to how it is often used in popular culture. For example, when someone is arrogant and self-absorbed they could be described in popular language as having a 'big ego' or being 'egotistical'. However, in psychological theory the ego has a positive meaning because it serves as an effective organising function and builds protection for an individual by setting up ego defence mechanisms.

Blanck & Blanck, (1979) map the evolution of the term ego since Freud's structural theory of *The Ego and the Id* in 1923. They propose a unifying statement that:

> the ego is an innate capacity to organise mental processes into a coherent form; at the outset organisation takes place in affectively charged islands of experience with the infant employing whatever apparatus are at the time available; and that qualitative change can be observed in the child when peaks of development have been attained (ibid., p23).

In the early stages of life, the infant's ego provides a container for the Self and a way of being in the world (Benson, 2013). At this level of identification, ego is Self unconscious to itself (ibid.). The Self is identified at a pre-personal level of ego development at which the infant is unconscious to the Self.

There is still a direct relationship between the embodied Self and transpersonal Self, which is an unconscious connection. Over time, as the individual grows and develops, the conscious connection between embodied and transpersonal Self is built through the expansion of the field of 'I' consciousness (Evans, 2018).

The incarnated Self surrenders to parents to be 'Temporal Guardians of the Self' and provide sanctuary with an outer womb that will soothe and protect the Being (Evans, 2017). The Self needs protection and nurturing provided by external 'unifying centres' such as parents, guardians and family members to survive and thrive (Firman & Gila, 1997). I acknowledge the variety of different caregivers that can take this role and for the purpose of this book I refer to primary caregivers as 'parents'. The infant develops parental imagos, which are 'primitive introjected images' of the parents set up in the mind as part of normal development and which remain as active constituents of unconscious mental life (Strachey, 1934).

If the infant has a positive experience of knowing that they are loved, that they can survive and are seen by others for who they actually are, then the parental imagos will be a source of strength and empowerment throughout their lives (Evans, 2017). For the embodied Self to have a valuing, respectful, protecting and soothing experience is a prerequisite for a healthy individuation process (ibid.). Later on in life these external unifying centres can be teachers, mentors, role models and therapists.

Winnicott (1965) described the essential nature of 'mirroring' as an empathic connection created when parents provide 'good enough mothering' by gazing at the infant and recognising them as a unique individual human being. This mirroring helps the infant feel loved, safe and secure and the 'good-enough mother' "meets the omnipotence of the infant and to some extent makes sense of it" (ibid., p145). Winnicott proposed that when an infant has an experience of appropriate, healthy 'holding environment' of mirroring and soothing by the parents, they develop ego strength and ego constancy, which means the individual has a sense of 'going on being'. He described how the individual can then experience their 'True Self' which can be creative and feel real (ibid.).

Winnicott's ideas were ground-breaking at the time, but he does not use the term Self in a psychospiritual context. To be clear, the difference in psychosynthesis is that there is a direct unconscious continuum between the embodied Self and transpersonal Self (Evans, 2018). The Self makes an unconscious choice to surrender consciousness and begin life's journey by identifying with ego. It is not that the continuum between embodied Self and transpersonal Self has been severed by Self, but it is the identification of Self with the ego that has severed the conscious connection between the 'I' and the Self (ibid.).

As the infant experiences a healthy 'holding environment' the ego becomes a stronger container for the Self. As the field of 'I' consciousness expands, and the will evolves, the individual is able to develop a healthy internal unifying centre (Evans, 2007). As this conscious connection between 'I' and Self develops, the individual builds enough sense of autonomy and identity to go out in the world without the protection of the ego defence mechanisms (Evans, 2018).

In contrast, primal wounding can be caused by empathic failure of the parents who treat the individual as an object rather than as a unique and valuable Being (Firman & Gila, 1997). Buber (1958) explains that when an infant is treated as an object it creates a cold, impersonal '*I-It*' experience rather than an empathic '*I-Thou*' experience. When there is an absence of a healthy 'holding environment' and no accurate parental mirroring and soothing then the infant's Self is identified with an ego that does not experience a sense of 'going on being' (Winnicott, 1965).

Balint (1968) described how this failure of fit between the needs of the child and the response of the mother leads to a 'basic fault', which the individual feels as a sense of something missing inside them. This disturbing experience has also been called a sense of 'non-being' (Evans, 2007). The experience for the individual is as if they have no sense of existing at all and the resulting annihilation anxiety feels like a living death, often reported to feel worse than actual death.

The infant's ego provides coping strategies in the form of defence mechanisms, for example repression and denial, to protect them from this excruciating experience of 'non-being'. Winnicott (1965) described how the ego defences create a 'False Self' for the individual, which results in feeling unreal, sense of futility with lack of creative play, spontaneity and use of symbols (ibid.). In psychosynthesis the 'False Self' is known as the 'adaptive survival personality'. I will expand on this further in the section on Soul Trauma.

Existential Wound

Traditional psychotherapeutic 'talking cures', such as the psychoanalysis and psychodynamic approaches, focus on healing the primal wound. However, the aim of psychosynthesis therapy is to guide the client towards 'I' consciousness realignment with Self. For this, the client has to have a robust underpinning of ego strength in order to expand their field of consciousness to a transpersonal level. Using the analogy of dirty headlights on a car, it is as if an individual's history and subsequent ego defence mechanisms have splattered mud on the personality. The purpose of ego development work is to clean up the personality for the Self to shine through (Benson, 2013). In psychosynthesis, the work of the early stages of therapy is to focus on building ego strength, which is a progressive process. With each turn of the spiral through the lower unconscious the personality becomes a clearer lens for the client to see themselves as they connect to Self (ibid.).

Through this ego development work, there is healing of the primal wound. This enables the client to build personal self containment, i.e. 'inner ground', so that they open up to face the deeper existential wound, which occurs when the Self is directly experienced (Evans, 2017). As the client becomes more awake to experiencing 'I' consciousness, a sense of autonomy and capacity for independent thought, they are more able "to face the existential wound and the fear of non-being directly" (ibid., p2). The client experiences a 'breaking down' of the ego defence mechanisms that have protected them from primitive anxiety and fear of annihilation to this point. The client must have enough sense of inner ground and self containment to be willing "to risk the dissolution of identity, to become disarmed and naked before the Divine", i.e. 'I' realignment with Self (ibid. p2).

The paradox of directly experiencing the Self brings at the same time a heightened awareness that the embodied Self has to live on a daily basis within worldly limitations. Fundamentally the existential wound is the experience of "the subsequent loss of connection to the essential Self" (ibid., p2). Evans (2007) also refers to this experience as 'suffering of meaning', when someone realises the meaning of their existence and at the same time feels the pain of limitation between aspiration and reality.

To give an example, a male client comes to therapy who is usually robust and has been successful in life. His father has died and he is so devastated with grief that he has lost his capacity to function. In traditional psychodynamic therapy the focus would be on the primal wound; this client had an autocratic father who bullied him to become a bank manager rather than allowing him to follow his heart's desire to become a musician. Going over and around the primal wound keeps the client in the realm of 'neurotic guilt and shame' (Evans, 2007), which can also be re-traumatising.

The client became a bank manager because otherwise he would have felt neurotic guilt for not doing what father wanted and he would have felt neurotic shame for not being who father wanted him to be. However, using a psychosynthesis context the client is guided to realise his existential wound. He is an artistic, musical Self and, due to primal wounding, he has missed the opportunity to express this creativity in the world. His adaptive survival personality has 'trapped' him in a traditional high earning job, and he has commitments of paying for a mortgage and children who are at university.

Getting to this realisation is an extremely painful existential experience for the client, and most often they try to avoid or deny it as true. But what can be missed in therapy is that the adult client is no longer under the control of the autocratic father, who is now dead. If the adult client continues to abandon Self and blames father, then they are hiding behind ego defences of neurotic guilt and shame. They are not facing the existential wound, i.e. that the client themselves is continuing to reinforce the loss of connection to the essential Self.

The client has to face their 'existential guilt' that they are not doing things in the world that express Self and 'existential shame' that they are not being Self, i.e. 'I' is not aligned to Self (Evans, 2007). It is not that father has abandoned the client, but that the client has abandoned Self.

As therapists we could get caught in missing the existential wound as well. Clients often present at initial sessions by saying something like "I have days when I feel it's just too much, I just want it all to stop, and I don't want to be here anymore". A therapist might hear this as suicidal ideation and of course it is important to check if the client is planning to kill themselves.

However, with a psychosynthesis context the therapist could see this as the existential wound with the Self expressing a deeper calling to the therapist that "I know I am here on the earth, I also know I am Self, and I am suffering within the limitations that this embodied form provides". The question that the therapist needs to ask is "what is it that you want to stop - is it a part of yourself that you are identified with or the situation/environment your Self inhabits?"

I propose that Freud was hearing something similar from his clients and wrote about this in 'Mourning and Melancholia' (1917). Freud differentiated between clients who experienced melancholia as loss of an ideal object rather than mourning, which is loss of a loved object. Freud used the term 'object' to refer to the internalised image of a person, i.e. parental imagos. Melancholia was seen as pathological because the client was unconscious about loss of the ideal object; they know who they have lost but they do not know what they have lost (ibid.). The symptoms of melancholia are lack of shame, dejection, loss of interest and agency in the world, loss of capacity to love, low self regard, self hate and self punishment (ibid.).

Using the same example, the death of the client's autocratic father brings with it the loss of the ideal object. The client grieves the loss of a loving father that they always hoped for but never experienced. They longed for a father who would have loved them for who they were and encouraged them to be themselves in the world. It would follow that symptoms described as melancholia also refer to the experience of the existential wound, in this case the client's loss of expressing creative Self. It is this deep, intense existential grief of loss of Self that has to be faced in the experience of the existential wound.

Freud's ideas were a reflection of the consciousness of the time of a structural, scientific paradigm during the Industrial Revolution and as a result, psychoanalysis and subsequent psychodynamic approaches tend to focus on working through the primal wound with clients. It can be seen that Assagioli's concepts were also grounded in structural, scientific discipline and since then consciousness has evolved to be able to formulate further the field of transpersonal psychology.

The concept and practice of the therapist holding 'bifocal vision' on both the primal wound and the existential wound for the client are unique to psychosynthesis and this was developed further by Evans (2013) into a therapeutic framework, which I will outline in the next section.

Triphasic Model

Evans (2013) developed the Triphasic Model of Psychospiritual Unfoldment as a therapeutic framework that can be used to guide clients through their recovery. The three levels of the Triphasic Model are pre-personal, personal and transpersonal (see Diagram 2).

As mentioned earlier, the Self incarnates, becomes embodied and in order to have capacity to be in the world Self unconsciously identifies at these different levels of pre-personal, personal and transpersonal. The Self is identified but not aware and the therapist guides the client to expand their 'I' consciousness to see how the Self is identified with these different dimensions. This is what is meant by Self awareness (ibid.).

The aim of psychosynthesis therapy is to guide the client towards the third transpersonal level by helping the client to expand their field of 'I' consciousness and build awareness of the connection between embodied Self and transpersonal Self (Evans, 2018). Psychological maturity is the capacity to have Self awareness and will to act with independent thought and action as an individual, i.e. process of individuation (Evans, 2013).

The Triphasic Model is a therapeutic framework that helps the therapist during therapy sessions to see where the client' Self is mostly identified. For example:

- when a client presents at the pre-personal level their Self is unconsciously identified with ego defence mechanisms;

- when the client presents at the personal level their Self is identified with adapted survival personality;

- when a client presents at the transpersonal level their Self is identified with 'I am I'.

Diagram 2 provides a summary of how the client initially presents at each of these levels. During the therapy process the aim is for the client to experience an evolution of will over time. The outcome can be noticed in therapy as a change in presentation of the client and a summary of what the change looks like is also given in Diagram 2.

In Part Two of this book I provide an in-depth clinical case of an individual who has experienced Soul Trauma. I will bring to life the Triphasic Model by providing details about each level in terms of how the client initially presents, what happens during the therapeutic process of recovery, i.e. evolution of will, and a description of how the client changes in presentation. In the next section I will outline a definition of Soul Trauma.

Diagram 2: Triphasic Model (Evans, 2013)

Level	Initially Self is identified with	Initial presentation of client		Change in presentation of client
Pre-personal	Ego defence mechanisms	Experiencing undifferentiated & fragmented consciousness Experiencing oceanic oneness, in symbiotic mother-baby dyad	Evolution of Will →	Object constancy, increased ego strength & capacity for integrated consciousness Awareness of 'ego-Self' as being separate from mother
Personal	Adapted survival personality	Experiencing 'ego-I' in a struggle with 'superego' (i.e. internalised expectations of parents & society.)	Evolution of Will →	Awareness of 'I am I' Self knowing itself as separate
Transpersonal	'I am I'	Experiencing 'I' in a struggle with Self	Evolution of Will →	Self knows itself in its wholeness Awareness of being in the world and not of the world

Soul Trauma

For some individuals the beginning of life is chronically traumatic, and they experience Soul Trauma (Evans, 2007). Chronic trauma means repeated incidents such as abandonment, rejection, neglect, physical and sexual abuse over a period of time during early infancy and childhood. The embodied Self lives in a chaotic, unsafe, unreliable, unpredictable and hostile environment and has no experience of healthy external unifying centres as 'Temporal Guardians of the Self' (ibid.). The trauma of the sacred wound followed by these extensive primal wounds is unbearable.

Evans describes how the ego protects the Self by anaesthetising the individual as a defence against the level of pain that cannot be endured (Evans, 2018). This allows the Self to retreat from the horrific environment; the Self makes a choice to go unconscious and to identify with the ego defence mechanisms. At the same time the 'I' remains unconscious because it would be unbearably painful to experience the physical body that is enduring such events as violence, rape and emotional disturbance due to abandonment and neglect (ibid.). The infant is numb, does not experience being embodied and cannot know what it means to be in the world.

This protective response to the traumatic event has blocked the infant's 'I' from having the capacity to access any experience of the soul and this is what is meant by Soul Trauma (ibid.). Without access to the realm of the soul, the infant is unable to access the superconscious and therefore to progress in their development towards 'I' conscious connection with Self and evolution of will. In other words, the infant is traumatised at the level of the soul, personal 'I' and alignment of 'I' with Self. They remain frozen at the level of Self identified with ego defence mechanisms and in an anaesthetised state (ibid.).

The Soul Trauma experience is a sense of 'lostness', feeling separate from Self and separate from the world; a sense of not being able to be 'alive'. The protective function of the ego is a survival mechanism to escape from the unbearable trauma and at the same time reinforces an experience of separation from Self and blocks the individual from experiencing the soul. According to Kalsched (1996), this defensive self-care system, which in childhood protects the personal spirit, later becomes a self-harming prison. He describes these ego defence mechanisms as a tyrannical caretaker that says:

"never again will the traumatized personal spirit of this child suffer this badly! ... before this happens I will disperse it into fragments (dissociation), or encapsulate it and soothe it with fantasy (schizoid withdrawal), or numb it with intoxicating substance (addiction) or persecute it to keep it from hoping for life in this world (depression)" (Kalsched, 1996, p5)

As mentioned earlier, Freud's (1917) conception of trauma as melancholia was the loss of the ideal object and he was the first to describe the ego defence mechanism of 'splitting'. He proposed that the ego split in half and one part of the ego turned against itself. The resulting symptoms were low self regard, self reproach, self revile and a delusional expectation of punishment (ibid.). This manifests in the abused client who turns murderous impulses against themselves, rather than expressing rage at the perpetrator. Freud believed traumatised individuals did not respond positively to therapy because they could not form a therapeutic alliance and engage in a transference relationship with the therapist.

By transference Freud is referring to the client bringing past experiences into the present therapeutic relationship by constantly externalising introjects "in a sense being actualized so that they can be related to as external objects rather than as internal ones" (Sandler et al, 1992, p54). Countertransference constitutes the therapist's intrapsychic reactions to the client, including limitations in comprehending the client's material (Hoffer, 1956).

Fairbairn (1940) stated that it was possible to work with traumatised clients and described how their tendency towards schizoid withdrawal meant they had awareness of their inner world of trauma. He developed a more complex conception of the ego splitting known as the Endopsychic Structure (ibid.). Fairbairn described how the ego split into three parts.

- One part of the ego operates in **conscious** awareness and for survival purposes the individual needs to maintain a good relationship with the other person (object). This conscious central ego internalises a good external relationship with the person (idealised object) that helps them to keep in contact.

To survive the abuse, the individual denies, splits off and represses the negative and frustrating experience of the person.

The result is that in their **unconscious** there are two further split off parts of the ego (ibid.).

- One split-off part is called the **libidinal ego**, which is needy, dependent and has an internalised image of the exciting part of the person (**exciting object**). This manifests as the abused child feeling a pull towards the parent in the hope that this time the child might get their needs met (ibid.).

- The other split-off part is called the anti-libidinal ego, which is angry at rejection, non-needy and has an internalised image of the rejecting part of the person (rejecting object). This manifests as the abused child withdrawing away from the parent, denying they have needs and sabotaging their expression of need to the person, i.e. an internal saboteur (ibid.).

Fairbairn describes how the traumatised individual has a trancelike submission, worshipping loyalty and excitement towards an abusive person who is in reality intimidating, rejecting, frustrating and disappointing (ibid.). This trancelike, anaesthetised state of the individual refers to the ego defence mechanism of dissociation, which accompanies denial, splitting and repression.

Since this seminal work of Fairbairn, other theorists have described similar splitting and regression in traumatised clients. As mentioned earlier, Winnicott (1965) described client's having a 'False Self' that they present in therapy and a hidden 'True Self'. He cautions therapists who sometimes mistakenly attempt therapy with a client's False Self. Winnicott describes a male client who could not truly begin therapy until he acknowledged his sense of non-existence, i.e. the experience of the False Self (ibid.). The client presented in therapy with a False Self that was like a nurse bringing a baby to the doctor to be spoken about. Winnicott believed that the 'nurse' False Self would wait until it felt safe and they could trust the therapist before bringing the vulnerable 'baby' True Self to be present in therapy (ibid.).

Kohut & Wolf (1986) outline their theory of narcissism as a vertical split, with one part of the personality that is seen in the world and the vulnerable split off and repressed part that is hidden. They were a strong advocate for the possibility of working with clients who had defensive narcissistic structures, which is the case with chronically traumatised clients. Kohut & Wolf identified a specific type of transference relationship between client and therapist, known as idealised and grandiose transference and described how the therapist can work with these clients being aware of the nature of their corresponding idealised and grandiose countertransference (ibid.). I will describe this in more detail in the Part Two of this book.

Recent developments in neuroscience reveal the impact of childhood trauma on the brain and physiological system. Van der Hart et al (2006) developed a model of Structural Dissociation of the Personality and, in a similar way to Fairbairn, they describe that individuals have a conscious 'Apparently Normal Part' and within their unconscious they have a multitude of split-off repressed parts known as 'Emotional Parts' (ibid.). In addition, other researchers have described similar models of split-off parts and a sensorimotor approach to understanding and treating chronically traumatised clients (e.g. Levine 1997, Ogden et al 2006, Fisher 2017).

My view is that these theorists are describing a similar understanding of the inner world of the chronically traumatised individual using different terminology. They conclude that the individual experiences dissociation (anaesthetising) and ego splitting that results in a part of the personality that operates in the world to some extent and additionally has a repressed, fragmented inner world of different parts.

The language used from a psychosynthesis context is that the individual has an 'Inner Child' that has two aspects. When a client has experienced Soul Trauma their 'Child of Self' is split off, denied and repressed so that Self is protected from the trauma. The individual develops a 'Child of History' that operates to some extent in the world. In order to survive in the hostile environment, the 'Child of History' develops an 'adaptive survival personality', which consists of separate split-off parts of the personality that are called 'subpersonalities'.

Psychosynthesis brings a unique psychospiritual context of the Self to understand Soul Trauma and holds a different ontological context of identity, i.e. belief in the nature of being. Schwartz-Salant (1982) provides a clear definition of the difference in ontological context as follows:

- Psychoanalysts (e.g. Freud, Fairbairn, Winnicott) believe that an individual's identity is located in the ego.

- Self Psychologists (e.g. Kohut & Wolf) used the concept of Self and believe identity is both within the ego and also outside the ego as Self. However, by Self they mean the whole person, not a transcendent or transpersonal, spiritual Self.

- Jungian Analysts (e.g. Kalshed and Schwartz-Salant) use the concept of Self to define identity and believe that Self is an archetypal energy from the collective unconscious.

In contrast:

- Psychosynthesis therapists use the concept of Self to define identity and believe the transpersonal Self and embodied Self are all one thing. The Self is both everything and also the Self is no-thing (Evans, 2007) and the Self remains "stable, unmoving, unchanging" (Assagioli, 1988, p26). In order to become something, and to know itself, the Self incarnates and becomes embodied (Evans, 2007). The Self expresses itself through identification with body, feelings, mind and personality. The Self becomes more aware of itself through expansion of consciousness and evolution of will. The phases of this developmental process involve the Self being identified at three levels of pre-personal ego development, personal 'I', and transpersonal 'I' aligned to Self (ibid.).

The Jungian Analysts hold the closest ontological context of Self to that which is held in psychosynthesis. In particular, Schwartz-Salant's (1982) work on 'Narcissism and Character Transformation' and his conception of Persephone as the split-off and repressed feminine Self. He links together the mythology of Narcissus and Persephone and outlines two stages of recovery; the transformation of the masculine (narcissistic structures) and the emergence of feminine power (split-off feminine Self) (ibid.).

However, I would argue that Schwartz-Salant's (1982) theory is limited because most of his book focuses on the transformation of narcissistic structures. There is a short section on emergence of feminine power that outlines the myth of Persephone, but he does not go into much detail about the psychotherapeutic process and impact on client. In addition, Schwartz-Salant does not cover what the recovery process looks like or how the client is transformed after treatment. The myth focuses mostly on Demeter, but he does not refer to Demeter in his analysis. He also describes the joyful child and masochistic child but does not mention the parallels this has to the myth in terms of how Persephone and Demeter were both self harming and there was little joy, even in their reunion.

The work of Schwartz-Salant (1982) inspired me to use the myth of Persephone to illustrate the psychosynthesis concept of Soul Trauma. I propose that the Triphasic Model of Psychospiritual Unfoldment is a wider and deeper framework covering all levels of recovery from Soul Trauma. In the remainder of this book I will present a clinical case study about a client who experienced Soul Trauma and a detailed account of how the Triphasic Model provided a psychotherapeutic framework to support this client in their recovery. I will refer to the myth of Persephone as an archetype for the inner world of trauma and an outline of the myth is provided in the next chapter.

PART TWO

BRINGING THEORY TO LIFE

2. THE STORY OF PERSEPHONE

There are many versions of the myth of Persephone and I base my outline of the story on two versions, Turnbull (2010, p19-26) and Shinoda Boden, (2014, p168-171). I have combined these together to draw out the key aspects of the myth.

Persephone was a beautiful young maiden and daughter of Demeter, the Goddess of Grain who caused the harvest to ripen and taught man to tend the earth (Turnbull, 2010). One day Persephone was out gathering flowers and strayed away from her mother to pick some narcissus. As she reached for the beautiful flower the ground split open and Hades emerged on his golden chariot (Shinoda Boden, 2014). He abducted Persephone, plunged her into the abyss, and banished her underground. Hades raped Persephone and made her rule alongside him as Queen of the Underworld.

Demeter heard the echoes of Persephone's cries and rushed to find her. She wandered the earth searching for her daughter for nine days. She did not rest, wash, eat or drink in her frantic search. She was inconsolable in her grief and fear for her child. On the tenth day Demeter found out from Helios, God of Sun, that her daughter had been abducted and raped by Hades and this was sanctioned by Zeus. Demeter's outrage and sense of betrayal resulted in her leaving Mount Olympus.

Demeter wandered the earth dressed as an old woman until she reached Eleusis where she became the nursemaid of Demophoon, who was the baby son of Metanira. Under Demeter's care Demophoon grew up like a God. She fed him ambrosia and secretly attempted to make him immortal by holding him in a fire. One day Metanira walked in to witness this and screamed out in fear for her son. Demeter reacted with fury, berated Metanira for her stupidity, and revealed her divine beauty as a Goddess.

Demeter demanded a temple be constructed in her honour, where she sat alone with her grief and refused to function. She "howled and tore her hair and cursed the land as ungrateful and undeserving of the gift of grain" (Turnbull, 2010, p22). She scorched the land, caused violent rain to destroy the seeds and broke the ploughs. Demeter was enraged against the Gods and rose to Olympus to protest; her fury was terrifying.

She threatened Zeus that unless Persephone was returned, she would continue to mourn, the land would not bear harvest and people would starve. Only then did Zeus listen to her and he agreed to send Hermes, the Messenger God, to bring Persephone home so that Demeter could see her with her own eyes and abandon her anger (Shinoda Boden, 2014).

Hermes went to the Underworld and found a depressed and fearful Persephone. Hades was anxious about losing his bride and offered her some pomegranate seeds (Turnbull, 2010). Although Persephone knew she should not eat or drink, she was thirsty and tempted. She ate three pomegranate seeds and Hades knew Persephone was bound to him forever. He let her go, knowing that she had to return.

When Hermes returned Persephone to Olympus, she embraced her mother and they were both joyful. Zeus asked her if she had taken anything to eat or drink. Persephone could not look her mother in the eye and confessed she had eaten the seeds. Demeter cried "Then you are lost!" and Zeus declared "your mother grieves and mankind suffers" (ibid., p26). Zeus ruled that Persephone had to live for two-thirds of the year on the earth and then return to the Underworld to be Hades' queen for the third part of the year.

When Persephone returned every year to the Underworld, Demeter mourned, the earth grew cold, barren and the seeds lay dormant. When Persephone returned to the earth the days began to lengthen, flowers bloomed, and leaves grew on the trees. The people on earth knew it was spring again. After their reunion, Demeter restored fertility and growth to the earth and provided the Eleusian Mysteries (Shinoda Boden, 2014). These were secret religious ceremonies through which people gained "a reason to live in joy and die without fearing death" (ibid., p171).

3. CLINICAL CASE STUDY

In this section I will use details from my clinical case Mary to make links between the myth of Persephone and the psychosynthesis context of Soul Trauma. The perspective I will use is that all of the archetypal characters within the myth relate to different aspects of Mary's inner world.

I will use the case of Mary to illustrate each level of the Triphasic Model therapeutic process. In reality her transition through the recovery process was not sequential and Mary often identified with different levels concurrently. For the purposes of this book, I present the levels separately to enable in-depth exploration of the dynamics of the Triphasic Model.

Client Biography

Mary is a middle age woman who is married with two children. She began life in a rural mining community in the north of the UK. Mary was often left in the care of maternal grandparents during infancy. Dad was regularly absent, working for the oil industry abroad and mum worked full-time in a factory. Mary is the oldest sibling with one brother. Dad was self-absorbed, aggressive and violent toward his wife and children. Mum was mostly frightened, timid and submissive. Mary's brother had childhood illness that meant their mum was preoccupied with caring for him. Mary often courageously protected mum and her brother from Dad when he was violent.

Living in small rural community, her grandparents were used to having an open house, welcoming children and adults to call freely. Mary followed this open way of relating to others. When she was 5 years old, she was sexually abused by an older boy; a son of one of the neighbours. She told no one about this. Dad's job changed when Mary was 8 years old and the family relocated to the south of the UK, 300 miles from her grandparents.

Mary's family instilled her with a strong work ethic. She studied hard at school, was the first in her family to go to

University and she qualified as a teacher. As a child she loved nature and creative activities, but she decided to focus on maths for her career as it provided financial stability. She married a man she met at University and their children are now school aged teenagers. Mary works in a sixth form college teaching maths and business studies. She took the minimum maternity leave and from early infancy her children spent the day in nursery care. Mary likes to keep fit with daily visits to the gym.

Presenting Issues

Mary had been signed off sick from work and contacted me through my website for private therapy sessions. Her GP diagnosed anxiety and depression and prescribed anti-depressants. Her father had died recently and, although initially she was coping, as the months progressed, she felt overwhelmed and unable to function at work.

Mary was constantly tired, she was not sleeping and had lost her appetite. However, she continued to visit the gym every day and pushed herself to exercise. Mary was keen to return to work quickly so that she did not let anyone down. She was anxious that a long period of absence from work would impact their financial situation, but also admitted impulsively overspending on unnecessary items.

3.1 Pre-personal Level

How the client presents

At the initial session Mary talked very loudly and quickly, leaving me little space to respond. She was agitated, wriggled in her seat and occasionally kicked out her legs. Her eyes constantly darted around the room and she avoided eye contact. Mary said she had to stop working because her anxiety had become unmanageable. The worst incidence was that she had a panic attack and completely froze while teaching a class of students. She was worried that others would see her as weak and incompetent; she felt stupid for not being able to function at work.

I often felt bewildered and overwhelmed being with Mary. She was an educated and intelligent person telling me about difficulties in her work role and at the same time she looked very young, like a small infant. Her face took on the characteristics of a baby and her eyes were wide and unfocused. Mary seemed to babble words to me that were a string of undifferentiated consciousness. When I began to speak, she would talk over me. She was devoid of emotion and was matter of fact as she told me her terrifying family history. When I tried to focus on the content, I felt lost and confused. I sometimes felt sleepy and then I felt her merge with me, as if there was no boundary between us. The relationship between us felt fragile and I sensed that I needed to 'walk on egg shells'. She seemed like a startled and timid creature that had to be handled very carefully or she would make a dash for the door.

Hypotheses: Soul Trauma and Persephone

My experience of being with Mary in the early sessions was confusing; as if there were two different Marys in the room. One Mary seems to be functional and have will in the world, while at the same time below the surface I could sense there was another Mary who was vulnerable, helpless and terrified. The myth of Persephone and Demeter is helpful to illustrate how Mary was presenting with Soul Trauma.

Demeter and Persephone are both Goddesses, but at the beginning of the myth they are engaged in earthly activities. This links to the sacred wound in that their incarnation in human form represents them being both transpersonal Self and embodied Self. Persephone symbolises the vulnerability and helplessness of the embodied feminine Self as a young, beautiful maiden and she experiences a premature separation from mother.

This can be seen as primal wounding because she experienced abandonment and absence of a unifying centre, i.e. not being held, mirrored and soothed by mother. Persephone's detachment from mother and premature separation left her open to be abused by Hades. Mother is not available to protect her from further primal wounding of abduction, rape and banishment to the underworld. In this way, Persephone symbolises the feminine Self that is split off, denied and repressed in the unconscious of the individual who has experienced Soul Trauma.

At one level there are parallels between the myth and Mary's personal history of primal wounding. Mary did not experience a nurturing maternal environment; she became prematurely independent. She was not protected from father's violence or from the boy who sexually abused her. At another level the myth illustrates the internal world of archetypes that Mary introjected from her personal history and that became inner parental imagos.

Mary's Self identified with an adaptive survival personality (ASP) that is symbolised by the Demeter archetype. Like Demeter, Mary's ASP is a caregiver who looks after the needs of others and neglects herself, while at the same time continually searching on earth for a part of her that she feels is lost. Mary's ASP was unaware that her Persephone feminine Self has been banished into the underworld, i.e. split off, denied and repressed. She described the hostile environment of her childhood with no emotion. Mary's ASP was anaesthetised from feeling terror and made her unaware of self-harm, self-neglect and self-abandonment. She denied any negative impact of her childhood history, she idealised her parents and considered herself a resilient survivor.

This kind of splitting, repression and denial indicates that Mary experienced Soul Trauma. Mary's Self was unconsciously identified at the pre-personal level of ego development. As a defence against the fear of anxiety and annihilation Mary's ego used splitting, denial and repression as a survival mechanism. Mary resisted my attempts to bring a soulful experience to our work together by controlling the sessions. She kept me at a distance by not allowing me space, put me into a trance-like sleep, and merged with me to deny my separate existence.

My countertransference feelings shifted throughout the session from initial fear, then trance-like state of non-being energies, and sadness. Receiving feedback in supervision made me aware that this unconscious communication from Mary was how she was feeling, i.e. she oscillated between terrified, despairing and non-being, i.e. fragmented consciousness/oceanic oneness. This state of oceanic oneness and merger with mother is symbolised by Demeter and Persephone not being differentiated. Persephone has no defining characteristics and is invisible; she prematurely separated from mother but is not distinguishable as an individual.

Triphasic Model and Therapeutic Interventions

The aim of the pre-personal level of the Triphasic Model is the evolution of will to move from oceanic oneness, to symbiotic mother-baby dyad and achieve object constancy through ego-Self separation from mother (Evans, 2013). Mahler et al (1975) outlined the psychological birth of the human infant from initial symbiotic fusion with mother towards an intrapsychic separation and individuation. Normal development involves the child in a struggle between closeness and autonomy until finding an optimal distance in relation to mother (Benson, 2000). Mahler et al (1975) describe how failures in empathic maternal responses disturb and arrest this normal separation-individuation process, which progresses through hatching from symbiotic fusion, practicing, rapprochement to object constancy.

Mary displayed approach-avoid behaviour of the rapprochement child, which indicated her Self was identified at the pre-personal level of ego development. Sometimes Mary bravely discussed her merged relationship with mother, but at the next session shamefully retracted her statements returning to idealising mum. She oscillated between hate and love for mother and between self loathing and grandiosity; an indication of the paranoid-schizoid position (Klein, 1975). Mary used splitting as a defence against painful feelings of grief and loss of her good object, i.e. mother, and the terror of annihilation of abandonment, i.e. the dread of death (Becker, 1973). Splitting is an indication of a borderline syndrome, when an individual "cannot integrate good and bad self and object images but keeps them apart to protect the fragile good internal object from being overwhelmed by hostility" (Benson, 2000).

I experienced a 'push and pull' dynamic in my relationship with Mary. Sometimes she pulled toward me being needy and dependent; she said how much she valued the sessions and became anxious when I took a break. At other times Mary pushed me away with resistance to my interventions or with last-minute cancellations. As stated earlier, this dynamic was described by Fairbairn (1940) as the client having two unconscious split-off parts called the libidinal ego and anti-libidinal ego. Mary's transference relationship to me was that at times I became the exciting object and her libidinal ego pulled toward me in the hope that I will be the mother who will meet her needs. At other times her transference was that I was a rejecting object and her anti-libidinal ego pulled away, angry at mother's rejection, denying she needs help and sabotaging the therapeutic process.

I found Mary's behaviour frustrating and at times I hoped that she would end therapy. With the support of supervision, I realised that Mary controlled sessions in this way to protect herself from being vulnerable. Her behaviour indicated she was experiencing a high level of anxiety and terror. If I was to reject Mary, then I would be re-enacting the abandonment that she experienced in childhood. Fortunately, Mary's adaptive survival personality maintained a good relationship with me. Fairbairn recognised this as the conscious central ego that internalises a good external relationship with me as an idealised object, which helped Mary to keep in contact (ibid.).

In my experience, working with traumatised clients is challenging because of the complex transferential relationship and the client's ambivalent behaviour. In addition, I brought my own countertransference experience of having a history of childhood trauma. I found it extremely painful to be rejected by Mary, both her resistance during sessions and cancelling of sessions. I was encouraged in supervision to slow the pace down, provide an external unifying centre for Mary (Firman & Gila, 1997), and as a therapist be a 'good enough mother'.

Winnicott (1965) describes the role of therapist as a 'good-enough mother' being there to provide a holding environment, to encourage play and provide a corrective emotional experience. This requires the therapist to have a robust management function in order to be able to provide enough structure, be flexible when needed, be consistent, reliable, with clear boundaries and accurate mirroring of both content and feelings. Maintaining a clear frame of a holding environment with a soothing, calm and empathic presence gave Mary a sense that I was alongside her while remaining neutral. Once established the holding environment enables the individual to work towards having a sense of existing separately.

In addition, Bion's (1959) notion of container and contained describes how the therapist "becomes a container taking in and bearing toxicity; holding it and detoxifying experiences and returning them in due course in an acceptable form as food for thought for the patient" (Young, 1995, p176). This required intensive work for me in my own personal therapy. Gradually, I disentangled what I had taken in from Mary's that was really from her inner world, i.e. she had projected into me, as opposed to what was my own inner world of unresolved issues.

Over time, with holding and containment, Mary was able to build ego strength and developed object constancy. She was more able to reconcile opposites and renounce splitting (Benson, 2000) holding good and bad in self and others, which Klein (1975) termed the depressive position. In psychosynthesis terms, building ego constancy in this way enables the evolution of will to move from fragmented, undifferentiated consciousness of oceanic oneness, to being in symbiotic merger with mother as a unifying centre, through to 'I and my mother are not one', which starts the journey to selfhood (Evans, 2013). The progressive process of building ego strength enables the client's personality to become a clearer lens for Self to shine through in the world (Benson, 2007). The individual progressively expands their field of consciousness, there is evolution of will and they eventually connect to Self. The next phase of this developmental process will be covered in the following section.

The outcome of the pre-personal level of recovery was that Mary was able to return to work and was able to function effectively on a day to day basis.

Table 1: Summary of Pre-personal Level

Client Presentation	Understanding	Intervention	Outcome
Inability to function & overwhelmed Anxiety, agitation & fragmentation Numb, dissociated & merging Infant, vulnerable, babbling Matter of fact, no emotion Push-pull dynamic; detached vs needy	Self identified with ego defences Demeter adaptive survival personality Persephone feminine Self split-off, repressed & denied Oceanic oneness and merger with mother; undifferentiated consciousness Rapprochement, approach-avoid (Mahler, Fairbairn)	Therapist as 'external unifying centre' Holding & containment (Winnicott, Klein & Bion) Good enough therapist uses 'love' soothing and 'love' mirroring Relational, present & engaging	Establishes therapeutic alliance Improves object constancy Increases 'I' awareness & begins separation from mother Diminishes symptoms, improves functioning & returns to work

3.2 Personal Level

How the client presents

Mary described how she woke up at 5.00am every morning, worked at home then dropped her children at breakfast clubs. She visited the gym and then arrived early at work. Mary admitted over-preparing for lessons aiming for perfection fearing the children would suffer and being assessed less than 'outstanding'. Mary worked late, and her husband collected the children. She joined the family meal then continued to work before bed.

Mary constantly worried what people thought about her and would ruminate with self-criticism and judgement after every interaction. She worried about financial security, but then her impulsive shopping left her feeling guilt and self-loathing for over-indulging. Mary filled her weekends with household chores and if she stopped for a rest she felt humiliating shame and guilt for wasting time. She would be angry at her limitations of energy and view any vulnerability as being weak and lazy.

Hypotheses: Soul Trauma and Persephone

In the myth, 10 days after Persephone's disappearance, Demeter finds out that Zeus, the most senior God, has sanctioned the abduction of Persephone. Demeter feels devastating betrayal and decides to leave Mount Olympus. She begins roaming the world seeking work as a nursemaid. In Soul Trauma, this symbolises the moment when the traumatic events have become so unbearable that the Self makes a choice to identify with the ego defences (Evans, 2018). This final betrayal feels is as if God has sanctioned the abuse; the primal wound resonates with the sacred wound as unbearable pain of the separation from God.

The 'Child of Self' is split off, denied and repressed and to cope with this excruciating emotional pain the infant becomes anaesthetised with dissociation. At the same time the 'I' goes unconscious (ibid.). Up to this point the infant may have some awareness that a part of them is lost and they may grieve and search, like Demeter. However, from this point onwards, the infant relies on their 'Child of History' to relate to the external world and to survive the hostile environment they develop an adaptive survival personality (ASP), which is symbolised by Demeter.

Demeter takes on the role of looking after other people's children. She overworks to produce a Godlike child. She dips the child in fire and feeds it ambrosia. When the child's mother screams in anguish Demeter declares she is a Goddess and to be worshipped in a temple. This symbolises the narcissism of Demeter who believes she is the only one who can look after the child. Mary had similar narcissistic structures and believed she had to be the perfect caregiver and educator of children in her teacher role. This was reinforced by the education system in the UK at the time which valued achievement in exams. Mary was feeding the children the ambrosia of education and dipping them in the fire of exam pressure in an attempt to create Godlike children.

Mary was unaware of the impact her Demeter ASP was having on her family and her inner emotional world. Whilst she focused on educating other people's children, she was at the same time neglecting both her actual children and also her 'Inner Child'. Mary had an internal tyrannical 'Hades' that acted as a protector and persecutor of her inner Persephone, i.e. split off and repressed feminine Self. Hades symbolises the defensive self-care system described by Kalsched (1996), which in childhood protects the personal spirit and later becomes a self-harming prison.

I propose there are two key qualities of the split-off feminine Self that are repressed, which are self-care (love) and self-protection (will). Repression of self-care manifests in the inability to feel self-compassion and self-love. Repression of self-protection manifests in the inability to feel righteous anger at the violation of personal boundaries and no will to guard personal boundaries. The parallel with the myth is that Persephone was forbidden nourishment of eating and drinking when in the underworld or she would risk banishment forever (Turnbull, 2010). However, Persephone knowingly ate the pomegranate seeds when she was close to freedom; she did not protect her boundaries and self-harmed to ensure she would never be free (ibid.).

Triphasic Model and Therapeutic Interventions

At the personal level the Self is identified with adapted survival personality (ASP). The client experiences 'ego-I' in a struggle with superego. The client's superego consists of the internalised expectations of parents and society. The individual works through this struggle and the evolution of will moves them from an experience of 'ego-I' to 'I am I'; the Self knowing itself as separate. This evolution of will brings a shift from pre-personal level "no will" to personal level of "I have will" (Evans, 2013).

The central focus for the therapist at the personal level is to call forth the 'I' of the client. The intention is to raise the client's awareness of the separate subpersonalities that make up the ASP, to encourage integration of these different parts of the personality and to help them build an internal unifying centre. This is particularly effective with clients who have experienced childhood trauma as their central defence mechanism is structural dissociation, which results in split-off parts of the personality.

When the client progresses from pre-personal to personal level there is a noticeable shift in their capacity to have an 'I' that is able to observe themselves as a whole person rather than in parts. At the pre-personal level, they may be able to see the different split-off parts of themselves in isolation, but very often when they are identified with one part, they are not aware that other parts of them exist. For example, Mary often switched between two subpersonalities. One moment her Self was identified with a 'perfect practitioner' subpersonality; she had a mindset that she was the only one who could possibly deliver education to these needy children, which I will call the Demeter subpersonality. A few moments later her Self was identified with a 'critical judge' who persecuted her for never being good enough, which I will call the Hades subpersonality. She was not aware that she had switched between these two, contrasting split-off parts of her personality.

At the pre-personal level I would mirror to Mary that I noticed she had these different parts and, in this way temporarily, I was Mary's unifying centre. Whereas, when Mary was at the personal level, she could see these split-off parts for herself and noticed when she switched between the 'perfectionist' and 'critic' parts. This indicated that Mary had evolved an observing 'I' that became conscious of how she had identified with subpersonalities. The evolution of her 'I' awareness laid the foundation for her to begin to choose to disidentify from different subpersonalities, which illustrates her evolution of will. There was a noticeable shift as Mary realised she had will and could choose to disidentify from unhealthy subpersonalities.

I propose that the mirroring and soothing by the therapist at the personal level has to be more 'will' oriented than the 'love' oriented mirroring and soothing provided by the therapist in the pre-personal level. This therapeutic work is similar to the transformation of the masculine narcissistic structures described by Schwartz-Salant (1986). At this personal level of therapy, clients reactivate narcissistic needs that were not satisfied by parents in childhood. They re-enact the same relationship from the past, now with the therapist, in the hope this time it will be different. Kohut & Wolf (1986) proposed that this narcissistic transference made treatment possible and they identified three types:

1) **mirroring transference** - client's narcissistic need for the therapist's acceptance of their ambitions. Client presents with grandiosity to exhibit their striving for power and success.

2) **idealising transference** – client's narcissistic need for merger with a source of 'idealised' strength and calmness to reinforce their idealised goals. Client presents with admiration towards the therapist.

3) **twinship transference** – client's narcissistic need to share important characteristics with others and to feel a sense of belonging. Client presents with longing to find that they have similarities of characteristics and experiences with the therapist.

When clients present with the first two types of narcissistic transference the therapist's countertransference may be to feel irritated and bored by the patient's grandiosity or to be seduced by the idealisation. It is important that the therapist is aware that these countertransference feelings indicate the client is experiencing narcissistic transference. The therapist needs to be aware of their own narcissistic problems otherwise they may retaliate when irritated or become grandiose themselves when idealised. It is more helpful to the client if the therapist provides mirroring to the client's grandiose transference and provides soothing to the client's idealising transference (Benson, 2007).

The 'will mirroring' at the personal level needs to affirm and appreciate the qualities and needs of each of the subpersonalities that constitute the narcissistic structure of the ASP. The 'will soothing' needs to have compassion and empathy for the client that they needed these aspects of their ASP to survive. For example, when Mary realised she had identified with the Demeter subpersonality of 'perfect teacher' I would ask her what was her earliest memory of this part of her, how did it serve her, what were the positive qualities? I would normalise the Demeter subpersonality saying, "this part of you has helped you to survive, it has been of great benefit to you".

In the same way, when Mary identified with the Hades subpersonality, I would encourage her to have compassion for that part that feels the need to punish herself and to see that there is some value in having good judgement and critical thinking. The skill as a therapist at this level is to help the client to see how these subpersonalities are also, at the same time, no longer serving her when they have an unhealthy impact. The key for the client is to bring balance so that they make a choice to identify with the qualities of the subpersonality that are healthy and not to become over-identified, which leads to extreme and self-harming behaviour.

When clients present with the third type of narcissistic transference, i.e. twinship transference, they are longing for a twinship experience as an affirming experience and to develop a sense of belonging. The countertransference for the therapist may feel similar to an earlier pre-personal level of the client trying to merge with the therapist. However, it has a different, sometimes subtle, quality.

It is important for the therapist to notice when the client makes a statement from a personal level of 'I' that either acknowledges they are similar to the therapist or to acknowledge that the therapist is similar to someone they were close to as a child. For example, when Mary was able to make direct eye contact with me, she told me that my eyes had a kindness that was similar to her grandfather. She then described as a child how she enjoyed walking alongside him in the countryside. They would walk for miles in silence taking in the fresh air and natural beauty of the hills and woods.

This was an important breakthrough for Mary because before this point she was unable to recall any positive experiences of her childhood and it reminded her that she loved the countryside. The twinship transference tends to occur later in the therapeutic process and it can be helpful for the therapist to disclose more of themselves (Finlay, 2015). When it felt appropriate, I chose to disclose my love of the countryside to Mary as a shared interest. The outcome was that Mary decided to stop exercising on her own at the gym. Instead she went for long walks and cycle rides with her family at weekends in the countryside.

Assagioli (1965) proposed narcissism is a psychospiritual disorder that occurs when there is a conflation and disruption of the I-Self relationship. The individual appropriates to their ego what belongs to the Self. The intuition of spiritual energy from the Self is correct but the person manifests this at the wrong level (Benson, 2007). For example, Mary has core values that disadvantaged children need educational achievement to reach their potential, which is the right intuition belonging to Self. Her Demeter ASP behaviour manifests at the wrong level of ego, she was often grandiose and un-empathic; she pressurised students and staff to perform. This became a maintaining cycle because her students had excellent exam outcomes, her narcissistic structures were reinforced, she believed her strategy worked and she intensified the pressure on herself and others.

Using this psychosynthesis context, narcissism is a disorder of Self becoming embodied (Benson, 2007). It is therefore understandable that traumatised clients present with narcissistic structures because Self is not embodied. Their main defence mechanism is dissociation, which anaesthetises the body; they are not fully living in their body. At the core of narcissistic disorders is extreme defence against relatedness with others and to the unconscious (Schwartz-Salant, 1982). Traumatised clients are therefore not fully in relationship to their body, to their Self or to others. Kohut & Wolf (1986) demonstrated treatment of narcissistic patients with mirroring and soothing, establishing a robust ego and, in psychosynthesis terms, a unifying centre of 'I'.

Over time Mary developed her capacity to disidentify from her Demeter and Hades subpersonalities. Self began to emerge when she realised that the values of the school did not align with her true values. This illustrates her evolution of will and her 'ego-I' struggle with superego. Mary moved from 'ego-I' to achieve 'I am I' through her realisation about her core values, which is an example of Self knowing itself as separate (Evans, 2013). Mary's will began to shift from pre-personal "no will" to personal level of "I have will".

The outcome at the personal level of the work was that Mary decided to leave the school. She was successful in securing a teaching role with a school that had values more in alignment with her true values, i.e. a more nurturing environment that cared for the whole child as well as exam achievement.

Table 2: Summary of Personal Level

Client Presentation	Understanding	Intervention	Outcome
Over-working, perfectionism & over-controlling Focus on 'doing' not on 'being' Impulsivity & self neglect Grandiosity & critical self judgement Anger, guilt & shame for vulnerability	Self identified with adaptive survival personality (ASP) Demeter ASP: narcissistic caretaker producing Godlike children in external world Hades ASP: Inner tyrannical protector & persecutor of Persephone (Kalshed); leading to lack of self-care and absence of self-protection	Therapist calls forth 'I' of client Raise awareness of sub-personalities Idealising & mirror transference/ counter-transference (Kohut & Wolf) Therapist uses 'will' soothing (compassion) and 'will' mirroring (valuing)	Builds 'internal unifying centre'; 'I' observes whole person not parts Learns to disidentify from sub-personalities Moves from "no will" to "I have will" Recognises superego neurotic guilt & shame Chooses to change job to align values

3.3 Transpersonal Level

How the client presents

Mary left her old school in July and would join her new school at the beginning of the academic year. Usually in the summer breaks Mary dreaded time spent alone; it was her worst nightmare to stop 'doing' and she avoided this by constant activity. This time it was different for Mary. She took some time on her own for 'just being'. She stayed with the feelings she experienced, tracked her awareness and brought this material to therapy for exploration.

She described feeling like she was in a dark cave, terrified, paralysed and trapped. Her body would go into freeze and she could not move from the spot. She described a darkness overwhelming her; a feeling of non-existence. Then she would break down crying; her chest and stomach heaved with sobbing, she felt nauseous. Her limbs would shake and tremble uncontrollably. Her head pounded and every muscle in her body ached. She would be exhausted and fall asleep where she lay.

Hypotheses: Soul Trauma and Persephone

In the myth Demeter had to reach a point of complete breakdown and rise up to Mount Olympus with terrifying fury before Zeus noticed her suffering. Demeter's breakdown began when Metanira discovered the type of care that Demeter was giving her son Demophoon. Metanira screamed out with fear for her son. Rather than feel shame, Demeter responded narcissistically. She revealed her Divine beauty as a Goddess and demanded a temple. She was furious with Metanira and denigrated her as stupid.

The outcome of this narcissistic rage was that Demeter found herself alone. No-one came to worship her. She plunged into grief and could not function. Demeter threatened Zeus that she would continue to mourn, her work would not be done, and other people would suffer, unless he returned Persephone to her. Demeter began to let go of her narcissistic structures by asking for help from Zeus.

This symbolises the beginning of Mary's breakdown of her ego defences. The reason she contacted me for therapy was that her father had died, and she was not able to function at work. She experienced a waking up of Self triggered by the death of her father. Her superego consisted of parental imagos that she introjected from her family system. As an adult she was still living in this family system that had not changed; the abuse was continuing. Her father often had violent rages towards her mother and on one occasion this was witnessed by Mary's children. After that incident Mary no longer had contact with him, but continued to support her mother on a daily basis. As long as father was alive Mary needed her Demeter ASP to survive within this abusive family system. The death of her father gave Mary an opportunity to let go of her Demeter ASP and reclaim her feminine Self. Her bereavement and breaking down of her capacity to work led her to reach out for help.

In the myth, Zeus asks Hermes to bring Persephone home. Hermes represents the therapist who acts as the Guardian of the Real Self (Masterson, 1988). Hermes goes to the Underworld and finds a depressed and fearful Persephone; he witnesses her despair. This symbolises the capacity of the therapist to see the vulnerability of the client and to tune into the lower unconscious. The narcissism of the Demeter ASP appears in therapy as an 'inflated false self', which acts as a defence against abandonment depression, i.e. "not to feel the underlying rage and depression associated with an inadequate, fragmented sense of self" (ibid., p90).

Hermes is able to move between the lower unconscious of the Underworld, and the superconscious of Mount Olympus; to be with the Gods. In psychosynthesis this is known as the therapist holding bifocal vision, i.e. to keep one eye on the unconscious processes of the client and another eye on how Self is emerging for the client. Demeter chose to go to Mount Olympus, which represents Self awakening. She asked God to reclaim Self and God called on Hermes the therapist to be a Guardian of the Real Self.

Hermes is a temporary unifying centre and eventually he is able to reunite Demeter and Persephone. Demeter has to face the depths of despair that Persephone has lived in. When Demeter finds out Persephone has self harmed and eaten the pomegranate seeds, she wails "you are lost" (Turnbull, 2010, p26). This symbolises the existential wound. Demeter faced the reality of the abuse that Persephone had experienced; the abduction, rape and banishment by Hades. In her waking up she acknowledged the loss of Persephone for so many years. Demeter also faced the reality that Persephone would have to return to the underworld for a third of the year.

When Mary stopped work in her break between schools she accepted and acknowledged the excruciating pain of her existential grief, i.e. the loss of the feminine Self. She came into connection with the feelings in her body that needed to be released for her to move forward in her recovery. This illustrates that Mary was at the transpersonal level as she felt safe enough and ready to become embodied and connect fully to her inner world.

In psychosynthesis the moral imperative of an individual is to initiate an inward journey that leads to disidentification from narcissistic needs, dissolving the ego, surrendering to I-Self connection and undergoing spiritual awakening. To redeem the lost split-off Self we have to descend to "the sleeping 'inner dweller' and find the Being within awakening to the process of manifesting itself consciously into the world" (Evans, 2007, p131).

Campbell (1989, p19) describes the point in life when people realise "you've got to the top of the ladder and found it's against the wrong wall". The pressure to achieve has driven individuals to fulfil ego related narcissistic needs in the heroic outer journey of doing and achievement. They have failed to build an inner life, which would have guided them in life's goals (ibid.). "They are not at one with the Self; not being what one actually is" (Dürckheim, 2009, p1).

The inner journey requires the individual to let go of preoccupations with superego driven neurotic guilt and neurotic shame, relating to judgements perceived or real made by parental imagos, which fuel narcissism (Evans, 2007). Instead the experience of existential shame helps the individual to establish 'am I being who I am?' and the experience of existential guilt establishes 'am I doing things in the world that express who I am?' (ibid.). This movement from neurotic guilt and shame to existential guilt and shame is illustrated in Diagram 3.

Diagram 3: From Neurotic to Existential guilt & shame

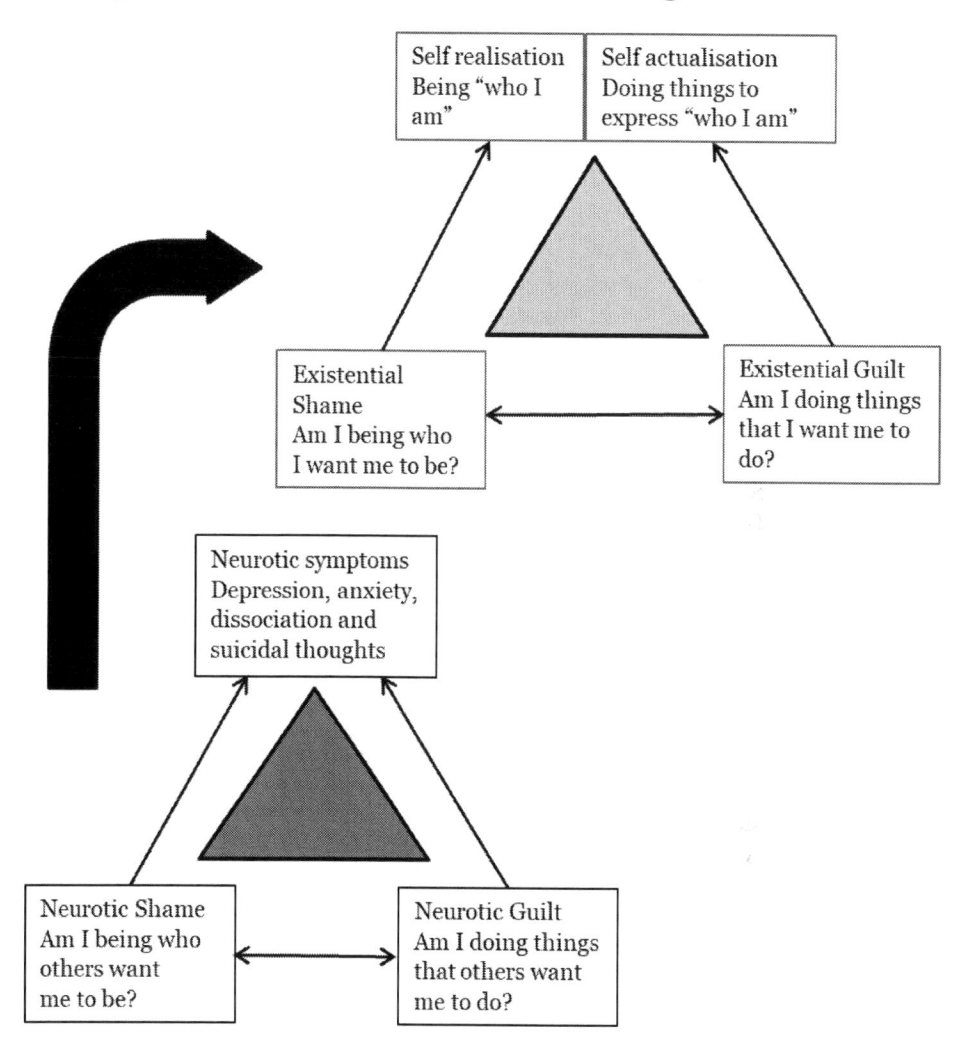

```
┌─────────────────┬──────────────────┐
│ Self realisation│ Self actualisation│
│ Being "who I    │ Doing things to  │
│ am"             │ express "who I am"│
└─────────────────┴──────────────────┘
        ↑                    ↑
         \      △           /
          \                /
┌──────────────────┐   ┌──────────────────┐
│ Existential      │   │ Existential Guilt│
│ Shame            │←→│ Am I doing things │
│ Am I being who   │   │ that I want me to│
│ I want me to be? │   │ do?              │
└──────────────────┘   └──────────────────┘

      ┌──────────────────┐
      │ Neurotic symptoms│
      │ Depression, anxiety,│
      │ dissociation and │
      │ suicidal thoughts│
      └──────────────────┘
         ↑            ↑
          \    △     /
┌──────────────┐   ┌──────────────────┐
│ Neurotic Shame│   │ Neurotic Guilt   │
│ Am I being who│←→│ Am I doing things│
│ others want  │   │ that others want │
│ me to be?    │   │ me to do?        │
└──────────────┘   └──────────────────┘
```

The movement requires the individual to participate in "an act of Will – a supreme sacrifice where one's life is dedicated to 'Thy Will'" (ibid., p131). As Greenslade (2001, p668) puts it "we are connected to the big story of who God is, who we are ... and what we are here for ... to 'image-forth' God's character and story. If you know who you are in the big story, you know what you're here for." In other words, your ladder is on the right wall.

Triphasic Model and Therapeutic Interventions

At the transpersonal level the Self is identified with 'I am I'. The evolution of will is the struggle with existential dilemmas between the 'I' and the Self through to the Self knows itself in its wholeness. At this level of 'I-Thou', the alignment of I and Self is experienced as being in the world and not in the world (Evans, 2013).

The focus for the therapist at the transpersonal level is to help the client's Self to become more embodied. This means that the client is more able to experience feelings and body sensations as important inner world information about how the Self is impacted by the external world, which in turn informs Self expression, i.e. will.

A client who has experienced Soul Trauma finds it difficult to access emotional responses that are held in their bodily sensations, due to the numbing defence mechanism of dissociation. From the beginning of therapy, it is helpful to ask the client questions like "what is it like for you in your body and feelings as you are telling me this?" This is helpful during the initial assessment to gauge to what extent Self is embodied and to identify at what level of the Triphasic Model is Self identified.

At the pre-personal level, when I asked this kind of question to Mary, she initially replied with a statement beginning "I think", which told me that she was mind identified. She could tell me the bodily sensations of her symptoms of anxiety and depression, for example "I feel my heart racing" or "I feel heavy and numb; I can't feel any sensations in my legs". Mary did not have a vocabulary to name the sensations in her body as emotions. I used mirroring to feedback the emotions to her, e.g. "That sounds upsetting" or "I can imagine how sad that would make you feel".

At the personal level Mary began to describe some associated feelings and body sensations that accompanied her subpersonalities. These usually related to neurotic guilt, for example "I feel guilty because I made a mistake" or neurotic shame "I am stupid and unlovable". When I asked about body sensations Mary would return to her symptoms of anxiety and depression, i.e. pre-personal level, and she continued to be mind identified.

At the transpersonal level the extent and quality of Mary's experience of emotions and bodily sensations shifted dramatically. This illustrated that Self had become more fully embodied. Mary began one session by acknowledging my interventions encouraging her to relate to her body and said that she realised "I am my body". This was a huge breakthrough for Mary. She came into relationship to herself at a more holistic level, i.e. mind, body and feelings, and often experienced intensive somatic discharges after a lifetime of numbing dissociation.

Ground-breaking neuroscience research described by Van Der Kolk (2014) has shown that the body holds the impact of traumatic events:

> "Since early 1990's brain imaging tools have started to show us what actually happens inside the brains of traumatized people ... overwhelming experiences affect our innermost sensations and our relationship to our physical reality – the core of who we are ... trauma is not just an event that took place sometime in the past; it is also the imprint left by that experience on mind, brain and body. This imprint has ongoing consequences for how the human organism manages to survive in the present." (ibid., p21)

Levine (1997) outlines a model for healing where the therapist encourages the individual to slowly discharge the trauma that is held in the body. The therapist supports the client to remain in their "window of tolerance" and to notice when external events or internal memory flashbacks, have triggered a re-enactment of the trauma resulting in a fight/flight response (anxiety) or freeze/flop response (dissociation) (ibid.).

Once the client has identified the pattern of their trauma re-enactment, they are encouraged to complete the actions that they were not able to do when the initial trauma occurred. For example, to push their hands out as if stopping the abuser, to punch the air as if fighting back during a violent act, using their voice to chant or shout out what was silenced at the time of the trauma (ibid.).

Mary noticed that in her deep despair she was trapped in a cave and unable to reach safety. She realised this related to her experience of being physical attacked and the rape, when she was frozen; unable to fight or escape. As her Self became more embodied, Mary was able to recognise that when she was in this frozen state she felt unsafe and she needed to self-soothe and ground herself. I supported her by introducing her to self-soothing and grounding strategies (see Table 3).

Table 3: Strategies for Self-soothing and Grounding

1) **Noticing:** Bring your attention to your inner world. Notice what is happening in your body, feelings and thinking.

2) **Focus on breathing:** Bring your attention to your breathing. Without changing the rhythm, just notice your breath.

3) **Regulating breathing:** Place your hand on your belly. Notice how the belly rises and falls as you breathe. Imagine a balloon in your belly and you are slowly letting air in and out of the balloon.

4) **Reassurance of safety:** Repeat statements, such as:
   - "I am safe" and "I am secure".
   - "What happened in the past is not happening now" and "I am OK now".
   - "I have will" and "I have choices".
   - "I have power" and "I am in control".

5) **Orientation in environment:**
   - Focus on one thing in the room that makes you feel calmer.
   - Pick a colour and name three things of that colour in the room.

6) **Calm Experience:** Bring to mind an image of an experience when you felt calm. Notice your feelings and body sensations as you focus on the image.

7) **Find a soothing object:** Locate an object that is soothing for you to hold, smell or listen to.
   - Hold a soft toy or stroke a pet animal.
   - Wrap yourself in a cosy blanket.
   - Smell an enjoyable aroma.
   - Listen to some soothing music.

8) **Physical grounding:**
   - Place your feet flat on the floor and press the soles of your feet into the ground.
   - Press your body into the chair you are sitting on.
   - Feel your 'sitting bones' on the seat of the chair.
   - Feel your back against the supporting part of the chair.

- Tap your legs and arms.
- If you feel in a safe environment - stomp, dance, kick and punch the air; shout, chant, sing and scream.

9) **Body scan:** Turn your attention to inside your body.
- Begin with your feet and toes, take time to feel the sensations and then work upwards to pay attention to different parts of your body.
- Take your attention to where there is any tension. Breathe into that part of the body and imagine the tension leaving your body as you breathe out.

10) **Physical soothing**
- Take a bath or shower and pay attention to the water on your skin. Smooth a moisturiser or relaxing oil on your body and pay attention to the sensation on your skin.

As Mary began to take responsibility for self-care and self-protection this signified the emergence of feminine Self. She acknowledged the harm she was doing to her physical body through overwork, over-exercising and lack of rest. Mary began to make healthy choices and learned at the 'point of choice' to listen to her body, feelings and Self before deciding what action to take.

At the transpersonal level, Mary experienced intense grief and during one session she described this as "feeling like a part of her doesn't want to be here". She explained that it was not thoughts of suicide, as she wanted to be here with her family, but part of her wanted to go somewhere that is calm and peaceful, away from the excruciating emotional pain she was feeling. This illustrated that she was facing the existential wound; she began to know Self as whole and the reality of the limitations of embodied Self. This demonstrated Mary's alignment of I and Self as she experienced being in the world and not in the world.

At the end of the myth, Persephone has to return to the Underworld for a third of the year and this symbolises suffering of meaning for individuals with Soul Trauma, who may struggle with accepting limitations of recovery at a transpersonal level. When 'I-Self' alignment has been experienced it can feel devastating that earthly triggers temporarily banishes them to the Underworld. Neuroscience research can be helpful in normalising this for clients and to highlight the importance of maintaining self-soothing and grounding strategies.

When the client is identified at the transpersonal level it is important, more than at any other level, that the therapist 'gets themselves out of the way'. The client needs to feel empowered in their recovery. The therapist needs to have patience to witness Self emergence when the client is ready and to be a guide alongside the client as a fellow traveller (Evans, 2018). The therapist affirms and supports the client's expression of will as it evolves at this level.

As the client builds their inner ground of emotional world, they can experience these feelings because they are more embodied. They no longer use dissociation as an ego defence. They are more able to access the soul as a bridge to the superconscious and their 'I' consciousness expands to become aware of connection between embodied Self and transpersonal Self (Evans, 2018). The process of therapy shifts as the client brings material with a more imaginal quality and they talk about dreams. The client is more open to the therapist using imaginal interventions and playfulness.

When Mary was at the transpersonal level, she brought a fairytale to therapy about Hansel and Gretel. She described feeling like a lost child who had been captured by a witch with promises of sweets to eat and now she was trapped in a cage. We explored this fairytale together and what it meant to Mary. She realised it related to the fact she had started at her new school. She found it difficult to accept and trust that this was a genuinely warm and nurturing environment. Mary said her new Headteacher seemed to be kind and supportive, but she still felt trapped and believed that any moment, like the fairytale children, she was going to be thrown in the fire and eaten.

I asked Mary to continue with the story; "how does the fairytale end?" She took a moment to recall. Mary realised that in the story, when the witch checked if they were fat enough to eat, the children tricked the blind witch by giving her chicken bones rather than their fingers. Eventually they pushed the witch in the fire and escaped. I suggested to Mary that she might be externalising her inner emotional world. She understood this and then had insight that she was the witch who kept putting herself in a cage and anticipating a life-threatening situation.

In her previous school her external world was hostile and matched her inner world of her 'Child of History'. She realised that things had changed in her external world; she was now safe. Suddenly, Mary said, "I need to push my inner 'witch' into the fire!" and was able to laugh with joy as she said this. In that moment it felt like Mary had hope for the future. She could give herself permission to stop being a masochistic 'Child of History' and instead to relish being a joyful 'Child of Self'.

This example illustrates how Mary made the movement from neurotic to existential shame and guilt. She was experiencing feeling trapped and waiting to be persecuted, but the reality was there was no one in her environment to be terrified of anymore. Her abusive father had died, and she had left her old school where there was a negative, pressurised culture. Her painful experience of inadequacy was existential shame. Her painful experience of not taking action to fully reach her potential was existential guilt. She was doubting and undervaluing herself. There was no one else holding her back and she realised she had no one to blame but herself. This realisation liberated her, and she experienced evolution of will at the transpersonal level.

Mary was more playful, imaginal and more able to access the realm of soul as a bridge to superconscious qualities of joy, love, compassion, warmth and beauty. She brought examples of numinous spiritual experiences in other aspects of her life. Mary was connecting more to nature and began creative projects at the weekend. While doing this she experienced feeling expansive, part of something bigger than herself, at peace and calm. Mary felt her heart opening in loving moments and joyful play when in relationship to her husband and children. She realised she had a loving family, good relationships with mum and brother, work she enjoyed in a supportive culture, and an inspiring spiritual community. Most of all Mary was making choices to self-love and self-protect, which illustrated that she had reclaimed her feminine Self; her Persephone.

Table 4: Summary of Transpersonal Level

Client Presentation	Understanding	Intervention	Outcome
Takes time alone 'just being'	Self identified with 'I am I'	Therapist helps client become more embodied	Experiences existential shame and guilt
Experiences feelings in body; 'I am my body'	Letting go of narcissistic structures and ego defence mechanisms	Encourages discharge of trauma held in the body (Levine, Van der Kolk)	Brings imaginal material & dreams
Dark cave, terrified, paralysed and trapped	Self becoming embodied & connect to inner world of emotions	Teaches self-soothing and grounding strategies	'I' consciousness of connection to Self
Discharges emotion held in body; shaking, trembling & sobbing	Experiencing existential wound: abandonment depression, rage and existential grief	Has patience to witness Self emergence	Knows Self as whole & faces limitations of embodied Self
			Makes choices to self-love & self-protect

4. CONCLUSION

When I was 12 years old my English teacher asked my class to write about a dream we had in the week. The dream I wrote about was this:

> "I ascended a spiral staircase and at the top found myself in a dark room. I walked toward an inner room that had a light. In that room I was met by figures so hostile and terrifying that I turned and ran away in horror. I fell through the middle of the spiral staircase and plunged into the darkness. As I plummeted downwards, I felt hands pulling me into the abyss".

Last summer, over forty years later, I found this dream in a school book and I felt sad to read my teacher's comment that this was an "imaginative story". I had dreamed about the hell I was living; my inner world of Soul Trauma. My Self had emerged in this dream, reaching out in the hope that my emotional pain would be seen, but instead my teacher thought I made up the story.

Like other individuals who have experienced Soul Trauma, I know how important it is to be believed and to be taken seriously. It takes enormous courage to trust anyone enough to tell them about the extent of the abuse they experienced. Carrying the shame for those who have harmed them is a core belief held by individuals with Soul Trauma. That is why the parallel between the journey of Demeter and the Soul Trauma client is so poignant.

In both cases they had to be at a point of breaking down to be able to reach out for help. Their survival personalities are so strong and competent that no-one would know they had vulnerabilities. Something has to happen in the wider context to trigger the breakdown and it will be unique for every Soul Trauma individual. The parallels between the journey of Persephone and Mary are summarised in Diagram 4.

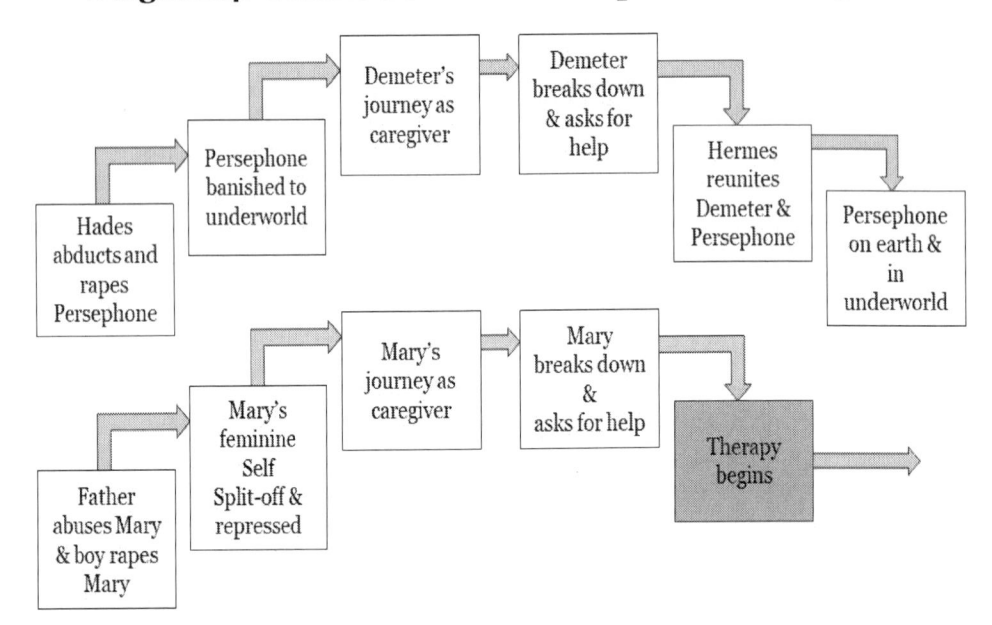

Diagram 4: Parallels between Persephone and Mary

```
Hades abducts and rapes Persephone → Persephone banished to underworld → Demeter's journey as caregiver → Demeter breaks down & asks for help → Hermes reunites Demeter & Persephone → Persephone on earth & in underworld

Father abuses Mary & boy rapes Mary → Mary's feminine Self Split-off & repressed → Mary's journey as caregiver → Mary breaks down & asks for help → Therapy begins
```

When the individual with Soul Trauma does eventually reach out for therapeutic help, I believe it is the quality of the relationship with the therapist that is the most essential element. It is important that the client feels engaged with, believed and taken seriously. They have spent their whole life feeling shame and guilt on behalf of those who have abused them. The last thing they need is a therapist who tries to pathologise them, which only serves to reinforce the belief they already hold that, "how I am is all my fault".

The individual with Soul Trauma is likely to be in a loop, whether consciously or unconsciously, re-experiencing their trauma in some form or another. It is not helpful to have a therapist who insists on asking the client to tell their story repeatedly. This merely strengthens the negative impact of the trauma on the individual.

The presenting behaviour of Soul Trauma clients can be challenging for the therapist. The benefit of the psychosynthesis approach is that it provides therapists with a model of bifocal vision to go beyond the client's story and presenting behaviour and to look for how Self is identified. During every interaction with the therapist, the Soul Trauma client is communicating the reality of their inner world of trauma. It can feel a huge relief to the Soul Trauma client when the therapist recognises that their adaptive survival personality is Self identified with ego defence mechanisms. Helping the client to understand this for themselves is liberating and can begin the journey to recovery. It gives them hope.

I believe the Triphasic Model of Psychospiritual Unfoldment devised and developed by Evans (2013) provides psychosynthesis practitioners with a solid therapeutic framework. The key aspects and unique qualities of this model, compared to other therapeutic approaches, can be summarised as follows:

- The therapist provides a warm, relational, encouraging and collaborative environment to build trust and enable the client to feel safe and secure.

- The therapist gives reassurance to the client by explaining how the symptoms they experience are a normal response to the events that happened in their history. Soul trauma is not the incidents from history, but instead the long-lasting impact these events have on their body, brain and nervous system, particularly the numbing effect of dissociation.

- The therapist helps the client understand they have come to therapy believing their identity is the personality that they had to form to cope with their history. The client has 'no will' and feels trapped by the pattern of behaviour and symptoms they experience.

- The therapist encourages the client to unhook from this belief. The client learns how to disidentify from the personality that they formed to survive their history; they have a history and they are not their history.

- The client explores the question 'if I am not my history, then who am I?' The therapist guides them to get to know their subpersonalities; the qualities and values of each of these parts of the client.

- The therapist listens carefully to the story of the client's current events and encourages the client to go beyond the story. The therapist and client focus on how the client's Self is emerging in the daily life of the client.

- Through an expansion of conscious awareness and evolution of will, the client begins to have a choice about which parts of their personality they want to identify with and express themselves through. They learn to disidentify from parts of the personality that no longer serve them.

- Eventually, the client reaches a state of realising 'I am I' and 'I have will', and can fully experience their emotional inner world. The client is more open to accessing 'the soul' and the therapist invites them to engage in imaginal work, play, creativity, and dreamwork.

- When the client has the capacity to access the soul, their 'I' realigns with Self. The connection between I and Self, which to this point had been unconscious, is now brought back into conscious awareness.

- The client can now see how events in their history had reinforced them to be a person that others wanted them to be, and to do things that others wanted them to do.

- The therapist helps the client disidentify from their 'neurotic shame and guilt' in order to fully unhook from the expectations of others who had an impact on them in their history, and who may continue to influence the client.

- The therapist emotionally holds the client in their grief as they explore the more painful existential level of shame and guilt; their experience of Self betrayal. This process guides them to realise 'who they want to be' and 'what they want to do' to express Self in the world going forward.

- The client is supported to face their existential wound; to realise the limitations of being in the world and not of the world. Even though they are now more aware of Self and have will of Self in the world, they realise that being human means accepting the frailty and vulnerability of the body, feelings, mind and personality that Self has available as a vehicle in the world.

Conclusion

- The client recovers from the inside out. They engage in processing and integrating their inner world experience. They are the only person who can know who they are essentially.

- The client experiences an expansion of consciousness to realise Self and an evolution of will to actualise Self in the world through independent choice and autonomous action.

- The role of the therapist is to guide the client and be alongside them during the therapeutic process. The therapist shines a light on the different aspects of the client's experience so that the client can see themselves more clearly as they connect to Self.

I hope in this book to have demonstrated how a client with Soul Trauma presents at each level of the Triphasic Model, to have provided examples of the dynamics of the therapeutic relationship and to have given examples of interventions that can be used by practitioners to support their clients.

Most of all I hope to have given you some insight into what it is like being someone who has experienced Soul Trauma, in the hope that readers who are practitioners will feel more confident, informed and equipped to help us all with our recovery. For readers who, through reading this book, now realise you have experienced Soul Trauma I end with some reassuring words. You are not alone, you are having a normal response to traumatic events in your history, and there is hope for recovery.

BIBLIOGRAPHY

Assagioli, R., The Psychology of Ideas-Forces and Psychagogy, *The Applied Psychology Review*, 1909

Assagioli, R., *Psychosynthesis: A Manual of Principles and Techniques*, Harper Collins, 1965

Assagioli, R., *The Act of Will: A Guide to Self-Actualisation and Self-Realisation*, The Psychosynthesis & Education Trust, 1974

Assagioli, R., *Transpersonal Development: The Dimension Beyond Psychosynthesis*, Smiling Wisdom, 1988

Balint, M., *The Basic Fault*, Tavistock, London, 1968

Becker, E., *The Denial of Death*, The Free Press, London, 1973

Benson, J., *Margaret Mahler's Work on Separation-Individuation*, Training Handout, Institute of Psychosynthesis, 2000

Benson, J., *Chapter 2: Ego Development, Psychosynthesis Psychology and its Professional Applications*, Core Principles in Psychosynthesis Psychology, Volume 5, (J. Evans, series editor) Anamcāra Press, 2007

Benson, J., *Ego Development*, Training weekend PT4b, Institute of Psychosynthesis, November 2013

Bion, W., Attacks on Linking, in: *Second Thoughts*, New York, Jason Aronson, 1959

Bion, W., *Transformations*. London, Heinemann, 1965

Blanck, G. & Blanck, R., *Ego Psychology II: Psychoanalytic Developmental Psychology*, Columbia University Press, New York, 1979

Buber, M., *I and Thou*. Translated by R.G. Smith. New York, Charles Scribner's Sons, 1958

Campbell. J., *This business of the Gods ...*, F. Boa & J. Donald (Ed), Ontario, Windrose Films Ltd, 1989

Dürckheim, K., G., *Practice to Achieve Man's Wholeness*, Training Handout PT7c1, Institute of Psychosynthesis, 2009

Evans, J., (series editor), *Core Principles in Psychosynthesis Psychology*, Volume 1, 2, 3, 4, 5 & 6 Anamcãra Press, 2007

Evans, J., *The Triphasic Model of Psychospiritual Unfoldment*, in: Essays on the Theory and Practice of a Psychospiritual Psychology, S. Simpson & R. Evans (eds), Institute of Psychosynthesis, 2013

Evans, J., *Guidelines for the Sacred Wound Term Paper*, Training Handout, Institute of Psychosynthesis, 2017

Evans, J., *Thesis Tutorial Discussions with Linda Hoyle for MA in Psychosynthesis Psychotherapy*, Institute of Psychosynthesis, January to March, 2018

Fairbairn, R., *Schizoid Factors in Personality*, In Psychoanalytic Studies of the Personality, Routledge, 1940

Finlay, L., *Relational Integrative Psychotherapy: Process and Theory in Practice*, Chichester, Sussex, Wiley, 2015

Firman, J. and Gila, A., *The Primal Wound: a Transpersonal View of Trauma, Addiction, and Growth*. State University of New York Press, 1997

Fisher, J., The Treatment of Structural Dissociation in Chronically Traumatized Patients, in: Anstrop, J., & Benum, K., (Eds), *Trauma Treatment and Practice: complex trauma and dissociation*, Oslo, Norway, Universitetsforlaget, (in press, 2017)

Freud, S., *Mourning and Melancholia*, In Pelican Freud Library, Vol. 11, p251-268, 1917

Greenslade, P., *The Big Story: Revealing God's Covenant Plan for Everyone*, CWR 2001

Herman, J., *Trauma and Recovery: the aftermath of violence- from domestic abuse to political terror*, New York, Basic Books, 1997

Jung, C., *Two Essays on Analytical Psychology*, 2nd ed., in: The Collected Works of C. G. Jung. Vol. 11, Princeton, Princeton University Press, 1969

Kalsched, D., *The Inner World of Trauma: Archetypal Defenses of the Personal Spirit*, Routledge, London, 1996

Kalsched, D., *Trauma and the Soul: a psycho-spiritual approach to human development and its interruption*. Hove, Routledge, 2013

Kalshed, D., Uncovering the secrets of the traumatised psyche: the life-saving inner protector who is also a persecutor, in: Daniela F. Sieff, *Understanding and Healing Emotional Trauma: conversations with pioneering clinicians and researchers*. Hove, Routledge, 2015

Klein, M., *Envy and Gratitude and Other Works 1946–1963*. New York, Free Press, Macmillan, 1975

Kohut, K., & Wolf, E., S., *The Disorders of the Self and Their Treatment: An Outline*, in: A. P. Morrison (Ed) Essential Papers on Narcissism, New York University Press, 1986

Levine, P., *Waking the Tiger: Healing Trauma – the Innate Capacity to Transform Overwhelming Experiences*, North Atlantic Books, Berkeley, California, 1997

Mahler, M. S., Pine, F., & Bergman, A., *The Psychological Birth of the Human Infant: Symbiosis and Individuation*, Harper Collins, 1975

Masterson, J. F., *The Search for the Real Self: unmasking the personality disorders of our age,* The Free Press, New York, 1988

Ogden, P., Pain, C., Fisher, J., A Sensorimotor Approach to the Treatment of Trauma and Dissociation, *Psychiatric Clinics of North America,* 29, p263-279, 2006

Sandler, J., Dare, C., & Holder, A., *The Patient and The Analyst,* Karnac, London, 1992

Schwartz-Salant, N., *Narcissism and Character Transformation: the psychology of narcissistic character disorders,* Toronto, Inner City Books, 1982

Shinoda Bolen, J., *Goddessess in Everywoman: powerful archetypes in Women's Lives,* San Francisco, Harper & Row, 2014

Sutherland, J. D., *The British Object Relations Theorists: Balint, Winnicott, Fairbairn, Guntrip,* Journal of American Psychoanalytic Association, 28: p829-860, 1980

Strachey, J., The nature of the therapeutic action of psychoanalysis. *International Journal of Psycho-Analysis,* 15: 127-159, 1934

Turnbull, A., *Greek Myths,* London, Walker Books, 2010

Van der Hart, O., Nijenhuis, E.R.S., & Steele, K., *The Haunted Self: structural dissociation and the treatment of chronic traumatization,* New York: W. W. Norton, 2006

Van der Kolk, B., *The Body Keeps the Score: mind, brain and body in the transformation of trauma,* Penguin Books, 2014

Whitfield, C., L., *Co-dependence: healing the human condition,* Health Communications, 1991

Winnicott, D. W., *The Maturational Process and the Facilitating Environment,* Karnac, London, 1965

Young, R. M., The Vicissitudes of Transference and Countertransference the Work of Harold Searles, *Free Associations,* Volume 5, 2:34, 171-195, 1995

OTHER BOOKS BY THIS AUTHOR

Working Below the Surface:
The Emotional Life of Contemporary Organizations.

Chapter Five: From sycophant to saboteur – responses to organizational change, by Dr Linda Hoyle

Chapter Ten: Clash of the Titans – conflict resolution using a contextualized mediation process, by Dr Linda Hoyle

Tavistock Clinic Series
Karnac Books, London, 2004
Editors: Huffington, Armstrong, Halton, Hoyle and Pooley.

Made in the USA
Columbia, SC
09 December 2018